"The world is made a better place each and every ordinary day by the millions of unsung heroes who serve others, sell and deliver great value to customers, and build enterprises that provide jobs, grow people, and secure families. *The Leadership Train* captures the heart and soul of this high and holy calling and will ignite a fire of unquenchable passion within the reader's heart!"

—**John Stahl-Wert, International Bestselling Author of** *The Serving Leader* **and** *Ten Thousand Horses*

"No one builds a networking business like Orrin Woodward. In this marvelously entertaining and easy-to-read book, he shares the thinking behind his extraordinary success. This should be required reading for everyone in the profession!"

—**Chris Brady,** *New York Times* **Bestselling Author of** *Launching a Leadership Revolution*

"I had barely started this informative and entertaining book when the next thing I knew, I was finished. Captivating as it is, it's actually a manual on how to build a successful network marketing business. Orrin Woodward is truly a master at his craft, and he provides answers to many questions here. Is there anyone else out there who wants to live a life of fulfillment? Then jump on the leadership train!"

—**George Guzzardo, LIFE Coach and Speaker**

"Reading *The Leadership Train* is like being a fly on the wall watching Orrin Woodward do what he does best: develop leaders who make a difference. If even just 10 percent of the people in our profession own this book, we will impact the world in profound ways."

—Dan Hawkins, LIFE Coach and Speaker

"I couldn't stop reading. Orrin Woodward has already proven to be one of the foremost thought leaders of the twenty-first century. Now he reminds us of the age-old adage 'Facts tell, but stories sell.' *The Leadership Train* is a fun fiction tale that demonstrates exactly what one needs to do to create financial freedom in direct sales, written by one of the greatest networkers in history."

—Ken Dunn, CEO of Next Century Publishing

"Hilde, Orrin, and I were waiting at a red light on Friedrichstraße in Berlin, and I asked Orrin, 'Can you tell us that thing with trains and cookies and cream again?' We all laughed because we had been messing around with it all day, and that is when we said, 'You need to write that book! It is a profound message that will help millions of direct sellers across the world get the business success they hunger for.' We are so happy the book is ready! We believe it will help our team to the next level. It will be one more 'mandatory Orrin book.' Thank you so much, Orrin, for the impact you have on our life and success."

—Hilde and Ørjan Sæle, Authors and World-Class Networkers

"Over the years, I have seen the potential of many people go unfulfilled because they couldn't frame their own doubts and fears and then overcome them. Orrin Woodward has brilliantly laid out the emotions that so many people deal with as they try to get traction and succeed and then systematically shown readers how to grow as a leader and win. Orrin has always stood above all others in understanding not just the science but also the art of building a community, and in this book, he has combined that wisdom into a clear, heartfelt tale of one man's journey as he builds the LIFE Leadership opportunity."

—Claude Hamilton, Bestselling Author of *Toughen Up!*

"Having worked in network marketing for nearly two decades, I have had the privilege and blessing of working with the industry's top field leaders, executives, and business owners, and I have 'seen it all,' as they say. I really believe that only Orrin Woodward could have written *The Leadership Train*. There is no more competent researcher or practitioner in the industry. This beautifully crafted and informative allegory will take you on a journey that will challenge every belief or misconception you may have had about network marketing as well as about yourself. Orrin lays it all out—the good, the bad, and the ugly—and shows us how he and the other founders of LIFE Leadership have eliminated the issues that have plagued the network marketing industry for years, essentially creating a whole new industry in which anyone who is hungry, honorable, and teachable can have success. Home run!"

—Tim Marks, Bestselling Author of *Voyage of a Viking* and *Confidence of a Champion*

"I can't encourage you enough to take the time to read this short story that has actually taken fourteen years to develop. The principles, techniques, and concepts you will learn will teach you how to build a successful compensated community. Not only will you learn about LIFE Leadership and be able to decide whether the opportunity it provides is for you, but you will also glean some golden nuggets that you can immediately apply to make your life better."

—Bill Lewis, LIFE Coach and Speaker

THE
LEADERSHIP
TRAIN

First Edition, October 2014
10 9 8 7 6 5 4 3 2 1

Published by:

Obstaclés Press
200 Commonwealth Court
Cary, NC 27511

orrinwoodward.com
lifeleadership.com

ISBN: 978-0-9904243-8-3

Cover design and layout by Norm Williams, nwa-inc.com

Printed in the United States of America

CONTENTS

CHAPTER 1

WRONG LADDER, WRONG WALL

I never know where to start!

Ask my wife. She's been listening to this broken record for nineteen years, and believe me; she points it out in a nanosecond whenever I get back on my rant. Frankly, she's tired of listening to it.

Want to hear what it sounds like?

"If I only would have jumped in on that two years ago!"

"Why didn't anybody tell me about this back when it would have made a real difference?"

"Was I in the bathroom when the teacher handed out the secret code for how to live well and prosper?"

I'm tired of listening to it myself, and now you probably are too.

As I have already made absolutely plain in these first couple of paragraphs in this, my very first journal entry ever, I also have a few problems in the *how* to start department. And let's add *when* to start just to round out the list of stuff I haven't mastered.

I have struggled my whole lifetime with knowing *where* to start, *how* to start, and *when* to start. And what's the result of this lifetime of struggle? I have messed around too long trying to figure out "the best way" to get stuff going. Often, I have jumped into things borderline late; I say "borderline late," but let me be honest here and just say that it's usually way-way-too-late late. And my life feels sideways and off-kilter from the momentum and trajectory that I thought I was destined for. I've lost out on a whole lot of opportunities, second-guessed myself continuously, and distracted myself repeatedly by staring jealously at other people who seem to be experts at success and mastery and accomplishment and satisfaction.

In fairness, I should also mention that I've also, from time to time, actually gone ahead and jumped into things and then not done what it takes to make them a success. That is to say, I've second-guessed myself *after* taking action just as much as I've second-guessed myself *instead of* taking action!

What an impressive start this is to my foray into keeping a journal. For the time being, let's just assume that I'll never show these pages to anybody.

But in case I ever do, I should probably mention that almost everybody I know thinks I'm one of the lucky ones. If you looked at the façade of my life—the degrees and job title I attained, wife, kids, salary, perks, toys, etc.—you'd say I made it. And if you told me twenty years ago when I finished my engineering degree that I'd make senior vice president of sales and marketing of a national automotive supplier, I'd have high-fived complete strangers for weeks.

But I'm not one of the lucky ones. The façade hides a massive problem. I'm stuck, stressed to the max, and nearly as far up the ladder as this ladder has rungs. I achieved all the goals I fervently hoped to achieve, and I now know that "this" isn't what I wanted. I jumped in where I thought the starting line was and got…nowhere.

Well, that's a bit of a ramble, probably the wrong way to begin my story and totally par for the course where my life is concerned.

Let me start this story over.

Pam and the kids and I flew into Detroit on Wednesday night, rented a car, and drove the eighty miles north to Pam's mom and dad's house in Davison. We don't get back to Davison all that often anymore, but Thanksgiving is one of the times we spend with Pam's family, and the kids will never let us break the tradition.

Thursday was great. I did my usual impersonation of a grand champion in a turkey-gorging contest and then recuperated with my father-in-law and two brothers-in-law watching the Packers play the Lions. It's a pretty big Michigan tradition, I learned many years ago when I first married into this family, to watch the Lions lose on Thanksgiving Day! Saturday, the Spartans were set to play. So Friday was just a hangout day for me, as Pam went shopping with her sisters-in-law, and our kids got pulled into a big cousin confab at Pam's brother's farm. Therefore, I had a lot of time to myself.

Pam and our kids love it here! That is very evident. Pam doesn't complain about the moves my career has demanded — the most recent one back to Dallas, my home-town — but I see what they have taken away most clearly when we're around her family. I'm an only child, and my folks are deceased. So the fact that we've just landed back in my "hometown" gives Pam and our kids nothing by way of family or community, not like here where brothers and sisters and cousins pull everybody into a happy whirl-wind. My career has pushed us wherever my promotions have demanded; I set my sights for the corporate climb and for twenty years have put other priorities aside. As I said, Pam doesn't complain (nor do the kids), and this almost makes it worse.

This morning, Pam sent me into town to pick up snacks at the Kroger grocery store for the big game scheduled for noon. Honestly, I felt dismissed…or not missed…or maybe better said, missing. Whenever I get a few days away from the relentless push of my company, I start to feel things that I don't otherwise. I start to think things.

And generally, this process of feeling and thinking — which I'm usually unaware of — takes a certain pathway. I get a few days to slow down. I experience the swell of backlogged emotions like a great tsunami of unwanted and unexpected grief. I find myself sliding into a medi-tative funk as I rehearse again the dead end that my life has become. And then, well, I forget the whole ordeal just as soon as my life gets back to its standard hundred miles an hour.

Today, as this story will soon enough reveal, was different.

Lumbering from aisle to aisle like a man in a drunken stupor, shoveling bags of potato chips and corn chips and pretzels, bottles of soda, jars of salsa, and blocks of cheese into my cart in near catatonia, I rounded the corner into the liquor aisle and rammed my cart straight into the cart of a terribly familiar stranger.

Bradford Henderson was standing stock-still. His easy posture behind his shopping cart, his hands folded restfully on the push handle, and his feet crossed as though he were watching a cricket match all suggested that he had been waiting for me. His eyes were level with mine, and a broad, warm smile animated his happy and expectant face.

"Still the man in a hurry, aren't you, Bobby?" With a different tone of voice, this comment could have been hurtful or intended as ridicule. But Bradford's face was kind, his tone was respectful, and the whole of his bearing suggested friendship and joy in the fact that I had just run into him.

"Oh my!" I stammered. "Bradford! Where have you been? I don't mean where have you been exactly," I hastily stammered, hoping not to sound like an inquisitor. "It's just that I totally lost track of you and frankly haven't heard a peep from you in over a decade!"

I'm just going to come completely clean here and reveal the background truth to my stammering, "Oh my!" Bradford Henderson shocked the automotive world over ten years ago when he committed professional suicide.

At the time, he was the youngest vice president—at thirty-five years of age—in the history of the corporation. Everyone knew Bradford was rocketing, straight-shot, to the CEO's office. His MBA degree from Michigan put him at the top of his class, and his string of engineering patents in the automotive industry made him the golden boy of the company. Whenever Bradford and I occupied common ground, which included a year of overlap at Michigan in our master's programs and four years at the same automotive supply manufacturer, Bradford was the one in a hurry. The rest of us worked very, very hard and were, quite frankly, both plenty bright and industrious. What Bradford did every day, though, was make us feel like we were standing still.

And then he quit! The future CEO of our company, the darling of our stakeholders, just quit. As I recollect the brief conversation I had with him the day he packed his stuff into a couple of cardboard boxes, I asked him if he didn't like the work. He said that, frankly, he *loved* the work. The shrug of his shoulders told me that I was way off the mark of his true motivation. I asked him if he was unhappy with anything in his life, and he said, "Bingo!" I think I used an expletive at that point. I asked him to please explain what he was unhappy about. His answer was incomprehensible to me.

"Michael Dell's talk at the Detroit Economic Club last year changed the way I view success. How does a thirty-one-year-old college dropout become worth over 21 billion dollars through online orders? Even if Dell is three times smarter and works twice as hard, it still doesn't add up to a net worth 21,000 times more than ours."

"He happened to be in the right place at the right time," I muttered.

But Bradford pressed on. "For the last year, I sought the answer to how Dell, Walton, Gates, and others did it. Finally, I realized they were playing a different game with a different set of rules by being *creators* (those who start companies) rather than *credentialists* (those who are hired to manage them). It's time to create my own business where I can promote myself just as fast as I can rather than waiting for someone to tell me I have enough credentials to satisfy the corporate powers that be."

He wanted to start a company where he could promote *himself*? Who gets to do that? The rising star of our company, promoted more frequently than any of the rest of us, was looking for more promotions because he was comparing himself to Michael Dell? The man who would eventually, and probably in relatively short order, get promoted to the CEO's office was looking for better advancement opportunities? It made absolutely no sense.

And then he disappeared. Personally, I thought he would settle down and be back, but I never saw him again. As I recall, his last words to me—which I found equally nonsensical—were, "It's time to see what life is like outside of the corpse-oration."

And now, all these years later, he was standing in front of me, his eyes level with mine, his face open and kind and at peace, and I could not help but notice his left wrist was bedazzled with a watch that to my very educated eye looked like it cost him at least fifty grand.

"How's Pam?" he asked.

"Um," I began, "she's pretty good."

Bradford's eyes lost a bit of their humor, and I had the uneasy feeling that he saw more in my answer than I wanted to allow. "And your kids?" he pressed on.

"Kids are good also," I said too quickly. "Really growing fast!"

The truth of the matter is that Pam and the kids are not all that great. Let me rephrase. Pam and the kids are terrific, but my relationship with them isn't. Pam is a soldier and, frankly, also a saint. I bounce her from place to place and give her far too little affection and attention. I know it's true. I don't want it to be. But the fact of the matter is that, at the end of the day or the end of the week, I am flat-out stressed, and no matter what I tell myself about how I will be attentive and present and interested in my beautiful wife, I get overwhelmed with the stress and impossible demands that I am constantly juggling. I am mostly zoned-out when I'm around my family. I mean I share proximity with Pam and the kids, but I'm not actually with them very much.

And so, since this little journal exercise is my effort to tell some truth, I may as well state what you can probably already surmise. My kids have a hole in their heart. Pam loves them wonderfully. They relate to me with a desire to be with me and still have some openness and show some vulnerability toward me, but I see the way their hearts are slowly closing off. I see the disappointment in their eyes, and I hear it in their voices when I promise to be with them and then change my plans. I know it's happening, but I do it anyway. Every time I let them down and see the anger and heartbreak on their faces, I vow to get my priorities in order. But, well, then life overwhelms me. I overwork, and I slide into my driveway at the end of another long week needing to be left alone.

Getting the picture?

"Work treating you well?" Bradford then asked. The corners of his eyes were crinkled in kindness as he sought a way to throw a line to me that I might hope to catch.

"Yeah!" I said too enthusiastically. "Work's great! I made senior vice president last year," I lamely added.

Bradford nodded his head encouragingly, walked around his cart, and gave me a slap on the back. "Way to go," he said. "Everybody knew you had it in you, big man."

This man standing beside me at the Kroger grocery store was not the same man I had watched walk out of our company ten years ago. That man was driven, dissatisfied, searching, restless, and as I have already stated, hard to understand. Though I would not have been able to put it into words at the time, I knew that he was on the hunt for something that he himself did not fully understand. Now, he stood beside me with grace and poise and confidence and kindness. Everything about his presence said that he was at peace with his choices and that he was no longer distracted by a hunt for something that he could not name. What I found unnerving was how absolutely *present* he was, both within himself and with me. I have met a few people like this over the years and have always wondered what allows men or women to be at home with themselves, comfortable in their own skin, and therefore completely able to be right there with the people they're with.

I must also admit that I could see plainly from his attire—and the gigunda Super Bowl–like ring he wore, as well as his wristwatch—that he had become accustomed to having very large sums of money. And this observation gave me a terrific pang in my heart. More truth: it was a pang of jealousy.

"So where did you go when you left the company?" I asked, unsuccessful in my attempt to keep the edge out of my voice. "It seems like you're doing great."

"Long story, Bobby," Bradford answered, "but the short of it is I found a wall tall enough that it made sense for me to stand the ladder of my life against it."

I'm sure the open-mouthed, puzzled expression on my face told Bradford that I had not exactly comprehended this comment.

"I know my actions didn't make much sense when I left the automotive field, " he continued. "But I realized that I would never be happy working my way up the corporate ladder. It simply would not take me where I wanted to go."

I just stared at Bradford, on one hand wondering what the heck he was talking about and on the other knowing too painfully exactly what he was talking about. Wasn't this precisely my lament? I never know where to start—where to place my ladder! Nor *how* to start, assuming I could figure out *where*. Nor *when*. And Bradford just told me that he had felt the very same way.

"So after some searching, I found an enterprise where the top of the ladder was at whatever height *I* decided it would be, where *my* efforts, diligence, and performance would determine where I'd end up."

I kept staring.

"And when I found that company, I knew in my heart that I had to be willing to let go of my credentials in order to create what I truly desired." Bradford's eyes bored into mine, yet his face remained entirely kind. "My logic was: Why not step off a ladder leaning on the *wrong* wall to allow myself to go and find a ladder leaning on the *right* wall?"

"Did you jump into one of those pyramid schemes?" I blurted out. I didn't mean to be rude, but that had been one of the rumors going around when he departed.

Bradford laughed joyfully. It was not a nervous laugh or an embarrassed one. It was a belly laugh, a good, joy-filled, happy laugh, with no offense taken whatsoever.

"The company I work with has been accused of being a pyramid by some folks," he said, his face flushed with warmth. "But I assure you it is nothing of the kind. As a matter of fact, the company I left is more of a pyramid because the only way to climb to the top there was to replace the people occupying the ever-decreasing spaces above me. Now, I coach leaders who provide real value to the world. When someone passes me, I'm ecstatic."

"When someone passes you, you're ecstatic?" I couldn't keep the sharp note of incredulity out of my voice. How could someone passing you be a good thing? In my line of work—in my *corporate* structure—being passed was definitely the worst thing ever!

"What exactly do you do, Bradford?" This, too, was blurted. And the second I asked it, I hated myself.

"Many things actually…I write, I speak…but I enjoy coaching leaders in my business best." Bradford's face was sincere.

"So how do you build your business? Recruit a whole bunch of people to get rich?" I asked. All of a sudden, I felt a creep of suspicion beginning to crawl up my back as I pondered the possibility that Bradford wanted to recruit me. I had that creeping feeling, and yet I couldn't help myself from asking. There he stood, looking like the type of success that I longed to be. And even though I was suspicious, I was very, very interested.

Bradford shook his head quizzically. "That's not it at all, Bobby." Then he extended his hand, smiled, and said, "Hey, it was great seeing you. Please say 'Hi' to Pam for me, and congratulations on your promotion." And just like that, he shook my hand and started moving to the next aisle.

Maybe Bradford wasn't trying to "get me," and I suddenly realized I may have cut this conversation short too quickly. "Wait!" I said. "I wasn't meaning to be rude, but there are so many of these get-rich-quick schemes out there. Seriously, though, isn't your business goal to go find people and convince them to become wealthy?"

"Do I look for people to convince them to become wealthy?" Bradford repeated. "Hmm. Interesting question. You know as well as I do, Bobby, that every successful company is only as good as its people. So I, of course, always keep my eyes open for top talent. However, my role over the past several years has been in coaching my growing group of leaders. This has kept me plenty busy, so I guess the answer is 'No.' With that said," he continued, "if you are asking the question because you are asking me to make an exception in *your* case, that is, if you are truly wanting to talk, then, for you, Bobby, I would make the time. I'm not sure if there is a fit, but the worst thing that could happen is I catch up with an old friend."

My head was spinning. I now knew that Bradford was willing to let me walk away. I didn't want to be suckered into anything, but I also didn't want to lose out on the real opportunity that he evidently believed in enough *not* to try to convince me of its merits. I felt as flat-footed as I ever have in my life. I knew this moment intimately well: sensing an opportunity to change my life and unsure what to do about it.

"Bradford," I began, a note of uncertainty in my voice, "I'm ten years behind you, and although whatever you're doing clearly worked for you, how can I know if it would work for me?"

Bradford gave it a moment, the warmth on his face as full as I had seen it during this whole conversation. "I don't think anyone can predict the future with that level of certainty."

He kept eye contact with me as he spoke. The kindness on his face was unwavering. And his entire demeanor was that of a man who lived by truth. He was telling me the truth right there, right then.

"I'll tell you something I learned along the way in business," he said. "While it's true we cannot predict the future, it's also true that if you want some things to change in your life, then you'll have to be willing to change some things."

Bradford Henderson smiled again. He clapped me on the back one more time. "There are no guarantees in life, big man," he said, "except the guarantee that doing nothing will achieve nothing. It was great seeing you, Bobby. Don't be a stranger. Feel free to reach out anytime. And do say 'Hello' to Pam for me!"

And then he pushed his cart on down the supermarket aisle as I stood stock-still in the middle of the oldest and most worn-out dilemma of my life. Should I call him, or shouldn't I? Do I want to go for this, or don't I? Maybe more to the point, *will* I call him, or, as with every other opportunity I've considered over the course of my life, will I quietly let this opportunity slip away too?

CHAPTER 2

WHIPPED

I sat behind the wheel of my father-in-law's car in the parking lot of the Kroger grocery store reviewing the conversation I had just had with Bradford Henderson, and except for the image of his diamond-encrusted Patek Philippe wrist watch (I may as well tell you that I have been a student of and luster after expensive watches for a decade), I had mostly talked myself down off this newest ledge.

My erstwhile graduate school friend and coworker in the management-training program of our company had made a massive mistake when he walked away from his golden career path! He had put on a good show back at Kroger, standing there in his sockless loafers, khaki shorts, polo shirt, and hard-worn baseball cap, the very picture of a man who is content, at peace, confident, and successful.

But the longer I reflected on it, the more I knew it couldn't possibly be true. Whatever sales job he was cleverly trying to pull on me wasn't going to work. I gave him points for not seeming to be desperate to recruit me. Yes, that deserved special points. But, I kept telling myself, his life couldn't have been what it appeared to be. And I was certain that I really was too far behind to try to fix whatever was wrong with my own life.

Having successfully silenced the voice of Bradford Henderson that had been playing havoc with my mind, I put my father-in-law's Buick into gear to pull out and head back to the house. Then I hit the brakes to avoid T-boning a bright black Platinum Edition Escalade ESV (yes, I've also been a long connoisseur of and luster after unaffordable cars and trucks) that appeared in front of where I was parked. The driver's side window was down. And Bradford Henderson glanced over from the driver's seat just as he passed me, his face lighting up one last time in a broad—and I've just got to say it: *genuine*—smile of delight.

"Really tremendous to see you again, Bobby," he shouted, bringing his Escalade to a stop. "I wish you all the best!" Two taps on his horn, and he gunned it, rocketing out of the parking lot, stones flying, suddenly transported into the much younger man I remembered, none of his boyish joy of life having apparently been lost to his years of work and struggle.

I say that I had nearly silenced the sound of Bradford's voice in my head (or was it the call of my life's destiny that I had managed to tamp back down?), but my little parking lot exercise of grimly reaccepting my fate was now lying on the floorboard of my father-in-law's car in tatters.

I don't remember the drive back to the DeVries' home. I don't remember carrying the snacks from the Buick to my wife's parents' kitchen. I don't remember who was there when I arrived, if they said anything to me, or I to them. I have no recollection of the Spartans game we watched as a family through the afternoon, where I sat in the family room, who won, or anything whatsoever about the rest of that day. My memory begins with sitting solemnly on the edge of the bed that night in the bedroom that had been my wife's from her earliest childhood but was now redecorated and refurnished with a double bed for the return of the grown children. My memory comes back online at the point where my wife was standing right in front of me, her hands planted combat style on her hips, her feet spread to convey a posture of militancy, and her face as angry as a summer storm.

"What is it this time?" she began. I don't remember when I've seen her angrier than in that moment. Oh, believe me; I've seen her *as* angry, just never *more* so.

"What do you mean?" I retorted—pathetically, I might add, though that is assuredly completely plain without me needing to point it out.

"We spend very little time with my family, Robert!" The use of the term *Robert* did not bode well. "And you know I have been looking forward to this for months! I need some human connection, for crying out loud!"

I wasn't ready to give an inch, even though I knew that in short order, I would need to give a mile. I simply stared back at her solemnly.

"And you spend the whole day acting like an eleven-year-old boy who can't spell *nihilist* but fancies that he is one—some adolescent who just had his Xbox confiscated by his parents for a month! Would you grow up?"

I couldn't completely stifle the small smirk that pulled up the corners of my mouth. Where Pam gets her references to nihilism, Xboxes, and the overblown existentialist angst of a hyper-imaginative eleven-year-old boy, I have no idea. She is a very bright woman, and though I was angry, and I knew also in deep trouble, her finesse with words made me smile. I really do love and admire Pam, even if I'm mostly lost in a funk and prone to being a knucklehead.

"Talk to me, for God's sake, Bobby!" Suddenly my wife's eyes flooded over with tears, and I knew my game was up.

I reached out my hand for her, gave her true eye contact, and said, "I'm really sorry, Pam." I don't really know how this works. A minute before, I was not sorry at all. But at that moment, I truly was.

Then I shook my head. "You'd never guess who I bumped into at the grocery store this morning." I made this statement with a sheepish and pained look on my face. I knew that the explanation for my behavior that I was about to give would not provide adequate cover or justification for the dopehead I had been all day. I soldiered on, nevertheless.

"Bradford Henderson was standing in the middle of the aisle, and I ran my shopping cart right into his, almost as if he was planted there for me to run into him."

Pam looked confused. "Where has Bradford been all these years?"

"That was my question exactly. But there he stood, for God's sake, wearing a Swiss watch that had to cost him fifty grand, looking completely at peace and at ease and, frankly, alive! None of the clawing, desperate, insecure, restless energy that I always associated with Bradford. It was all gone. He was just standing there smiling at me, and it was obvious that he is doing ridiculously well."

At this point, Pam's face changed expressions. Her eyes became hooded. Her mouth was twisted to the side in a gesture of, "Here it comes again." And a look of resigned weariness had taken over the whole of her countenance.

"He made you some kind of a job offer, didn't he!" The look on Pam's expression as she declared this was not a happy one.

"Actually, no, he didn't. In fact, he didn't even ask me for my number!"

Pam's weariness and suspicion only darkened. I had taken her down this twisty path before, and she knew all of its turns.

"You think his life is somehow better than yours, and it's kicked up all of that ridiculous insecurity and discontent that lurks inside you like a caged animal."

"I don't think that's fair!" I retorted. Truth is she had nailed it.

"But you did notice that fifty-grand watch, didn't you, Bobby!"

I flinched and felt myself quickly growing angry—okay, *defensive*. "I didn't tell you about Bradford Henderson because he was wearing a doggone Patek Philippe with enough diamonds buried in the bezel to stock a small jewelry store! I told you about him because he looked, well, *happy*!"

"But you think an expensive enough watch will make you happy!" she retorted right back.

"For Pete's sake, Pam, I do not think that! It does no good for you to throw insults at me!" True enough, I *did* think that an expensive wristwatch would make me happy. Well, let me refine that statement; I *knew* that an expensive wristwatch would *not* make me happy, but I liked what it represented: freedom from financial stress.

"I'm just trying to figure out," I pressed on, "how a guy my age leaves the corporate ladder and then runs circles around me!"

"So let me get this straight, Bobby," Pam continued. "You bumped into Bradford Henderson in the grocery store. He was wearing a fifty-thousand-dollar watch on his, let me guess, very tanned wrist, and, oh, by the way, he looked really happy and content with his life. Am I getting this straight so far?" she asked sarcastically. "And this explains why you spent the rest of the day acting like an eleven-year-old boy who enjoys a good, long sulk?

"Oh, and I forgot: he didn't offer you a job, and so you're not thinking about some wild scheme that involves pyramid building and overpriced products! Does that about cover it?"

"He said it's not a pyramid!" I felt ridiculous.

"Oh, great. It's an isosceles triangle, and you have no interest in joining his ridiculous venture. And if you did, you'd only have to recruit a thousand people to fill their garages with crap!"

Okay, I have on an occasion (or two) tried my hand at building a multilevel marketing company. I conveniently avoided mentioning this to Bradford when we had talked. And, well, I have gone a little overboard in those efforts, pouring my deep frustration into the fantasy of getting rich quick. And, yes, I promised Pam three years ago that I was done with that and that I would keep my nose to the grindstone and take care of business. And wasn't the fact that I had been promoted to senior vice president evidence that I was holding up my end of the bargain?

"I know that stuff never works," I said.

"Which is why you spent all day looking like a whipped puppy dog! You know it doesn't work. So you sickened yourself with wanting to do what you don't want to do because you actually *don't* know that it doesn't work, and, in point of fact, you *do* want to do it!"

The corners of my mouth turned up a second time. If there was an event for Olympic Sentence Structuring, Pam just got a string of perfect 10s!

"Whatever it is, Pam, it doesn't work!"

Pam's hands were back on her hips, her feet back in militant defiance.

"I don't want to join Bradford Henderson in his business!"

"Join him or don't!"

"I won't!"

Pam shrugged. Her face and posture said, "You won't, or you will; in any event, my opinion obviously doesn't count!"

"I won't!" I repeated. "I'm telling you, Pam, I'm not interested in whatever Bradford is selling."

"You told me he wasn't selling anything," she replied. Pam was not done with this fight.

"He *wasn't* selling anything—which is what was so strange, quite frankly," I couldn't help myself from adding.

Pam shook her head, a look of pained resignation taking over her whole expression as though my mind and heart were already fully made up to put her through another round of pure hell.

"Bobby, do whatever you're going to do! Join Bradford, or don't join him. Throw us down another rat's hole of distraction, or sit around and mope about the latest prospect that you don't have the guts to seize."

She just shook her head. "I'm tired, Bobby. I wish you would take the reins of your life for once. Make the decision to be happy with the job you have. Make the decision to leave the job you have and pursue some other dream. But in either case, actually pursue it! Act like a grownup and exercise the courage of your conviction for a change!"

My head slumped into my chest. Pam was getting to the crux of the matter, and now she was hitting me with very low blows — well, very fair blows that hit me low.

"No one has a gun to your head, Bobby," she pressed on. "No one's forcing you to go to a job every day that you don't want to go to. And nobody has your hands tied behind your back keeping you from fulfilling your life's calling, holding you back from your special destiny on Earth!" Pam was beginning to sound hysterical. Her voice was taking on a singsong tone of mockery, or maybe it was just pure grief. "I have been standing behind you, following you back and forth across the country, backing you to the hilt, and frankly, I do not deserve to be treated like some shadow that you don't have the time to relate to with any depth of feeling or consideration for what I might be going through! I know you have struggles, Bobby. But you don't seem to ever consider the fact that you have a wife and children, and we've got some struggles too."

I thought, "I *have* considered that I have a wife and children who deserve far, far better from me. There is little that I consider more than that, and I don't need my wife to point out my abject failures as a husband and father." But I kept these thoughts to myself.

"Pam," I tried one more time, "all I did was run into an old friend, which caused me to have some thoughts that I struggled with today. I'm not going to rush out and join Bradford in some grand scheme, alright?" This was at least the third or fourth time I issued this lame declaration.

Pam shrugged one more time. She didn't say again, "Join him, or don't join him," but her shrug was the equivalent of those exact words. She turned and made for the door of the bedroom.

"He was driving a brand-new Platinum Edition Escalade!"

Pam grabbed the doorknob, nearly ripping the entire door off its hinges, left the room, and slammed the door behind her with enough vehemence to almost tear off not only the door and hinges but also the frame right from its studs.

Yes, I was completely aware of the fact that I was an idiot!

CHAPTER 3

U-TURN

I waited maybe half a minute after ringing the doorbell, several times glancing around the spacious property that surrounded the grand house I had located with a quick Google search from my smartphone. Broad lawns stretched out to the four points of the compass, with verandas ringing the east, south, and west sides of the home. I could see a tennis court, a series of inter-connecting gathering spaces, a swimming pool, what looked like a traditional carriage house, a proper garage with four doors and a dormered second floor above it, and a beautiful stand of woods tucked in and around the handsome property.

I shook my head in amazement—and also despair. I pushed the doorbell a second time.

My drive north from Davison, passing the Holloway Reservoir, had been made in slow motion. The world had geared down its rotation, and my mind, though resolute, was almost in a dreamlike state. It felt like I was watching myself, like I wasn't actually living through what I was living through.

As I had driven past Lakeville High School, recognizing it from Pam's memorabilia and yearbooks, I felt kicked in the gut. Pam's high school. Pam's childhood community. Pam's life. I was slowly making my way through the landscape of my dearest companion's true home, and I no longer knew whether she was going to permit me to be a part of it, to be a part of her.

Deciding to point my rental car toward Bradford's home, my own suitcase packed and laying desolate on the passenger's seat beside me, had only been the most recent in a long string of boneheaded decisions. It was Sunday afternoon! Who drops in on anybody on a Sunday unannounced? Bradford and his family were probably enjoying a brunch somewhere after church. And even if he turned out to be at home, what was he to do about the mess I was in?

I shook my head again, looked down at my feet to give them their new instructions, and spun around to head back to my car. I had burned up an hour driving in the wrong direction, which was far from the worst part of my day. There were plenty of flights to choose from to take me from Detroit back to Dallas. I absentmindedly hit the car-door opener on my key fob, the rental chirping its obedience in trying to unlock its already unlocked doors in that patch of America that was surely a couple of hundred square miles away from the closest auto thief, and opened the driver's side door.

"Bobby?"

The voice didn't come from the main house where I had been loafing, staring at my shoes while pondering my doom. It came from the now-open door of the carriage house. Bradford Henderson's look was all question marks as he took in the sight of me.

"Come on in," he quickly added. "I was just thinking that a break from my little writing project was in high order. Want some coffee?"

I saw the hospitality of the gesture, knew that he just made it all up, and was glad to be looking at a door that wasn't closed to me. I walked away from my rental car, shook Bradford's hand, and was pulled into an expansive library where, by the look of things, Bradford was in the midst of writing several doctoral dissertations. A fan of over a dozen open texts surrounded a central, antique library table where, clearly, he had just been sitting, a sheaf of writing paper showing that he was midway through the draft of a significant manuscript. I hadn't remembered — or perhaps known — this bookish side of my once-upon-a-time engineer friend.

"How do you like it?" Bradford had a coffee mug in one hand and a fresh pot of coffee in the other, ready to pour.

"Black."

Black it was — and delicious.

"I love it that you stopped in, Bobby," Bradford began, his own cup refilled with coffee. "But how did you know I was home? I'd have hated to have you drive up here and find nobody home." He wasn't scolding.

"Well, true," I began falteringly. There was no way to finesse this story. I smiled, or maybe grimaced, and then continued. "I didn't plan to come visit you, actually," I started to explain.

Bradford waited.

"I was heading out, intending to drive south to Detroit to get back to my office in Dallas. But I made a U-turn and headed north instead."

The look on Bradford's face was a perfect marriage of confusion, curiosity, worry, and kindness.

"Flying back alone?" he asked, his face conveying compassion. Obviously, I was flying back alone. Either that, or my wife and kids were locked in the trunk.

"Pam suggested it," I answered, sure that my face gave away the anguish I was trying to hide. "She wants a little more time with her family," I continued, "and since she homeschools the kids, they're good to go." That seemed like enough said.

"When will she be rejoining you?" Bradford asked.

He had me there. When will she be rejoining me? That's the question I had just spent my slow-motion morning asking myself, the question clawing again and again across my soul.

"Well," I began, knowing that my face looked like pure hell, "that's just the thing," I continued. "I'm not sure when she will be rejoining me."

"Why don't you tell me what's going on, buddy," Bradford responded. "Come on; have a seat," he added, gesturing with his arm toward a circle of lazy boys. I carried my coffee over to one of the chairs and took a seat, Bradford joining me in the adjacent recliner.

"Can I just say, Bobby, that all marriages go through some rough patches? Heck, Chrissie and I spent several years in one."

"Well, thank you for saying that. Actually, I thought we were doing well enough. I should say that the last time I saw you, that's what I was still trying to tell myself."

"So something took a bad turn since I saw you?" Bradford inquired.

I shook my head and raised my eyebrows, not sure exactly what more I should say.

"I hope our little talk didn't contribute to any of this," Bradford then added.

"Honestly, Bradford, our conversation, yours and mine, didn't create Pam's request to have some time apart, though to be perfectly fair," I continued, "my visit with you probably brought some things to a head that have been going on for a long time between Pam and me."

Bradford was leaning forward, his elbows resting on his legs, his hands clasped around his coffee cup as though it were a talisman.

"Seeing you at Kroger set something off inside of me that has raised its head a number of times over the years of my marriage. You might call it discontent or self-flagellation or maybe even, if I can be honest, some jealousy." I found it strange that I felt so comfortable sharing with Bradford even though we hadn't been close for over a decade. It seemed right to be talking straight like this, and there was no evidence that he was taking any offense from my words. And he certainly was not flinching from the rawness of what I was sharing with him. "I've taken Pam through a couple of rounds of trying to jump into some things like maybe what you're doing, and I've given her a pretty bad time since I ran into you, truth be told."

"What does it profit a man if he gains the whole world but loses his soul mate?"

It sounded like an old saying from somewhere, but I couldn't remember where I had heard it before. Regardless, I had to agree with Bradford's sentiment, and I nodded my head so.

"If I'm getting this right, Bobby, the idea of you working with me set some things off inside of you that then set some things off inside of Pam, and she doesn't want you jumping into something with me. Is that about it?"

"Actually, no!" I responded. "I know that it could look that way. But Pam never objected to the dreams that I had or the business ventures I tried to jump into." This was true. Pam's problem over our years of marriage was never that I longed to do something bigger. She said it correctly when she told me that no one had a gun to my head and no one had my hands tied. I did not deserve Pam, for she gave me her complete backing over each equivocation of an idea that I had been possessed by and then subsequently abandoned.

"Pam's issue," I continued, "is the way I have blown left and then right, from one scheme to another, never truly committing myself to any of them or making peace with the circumstances of my corporate opportunities either. It shames me to say that she has always given me freedom, her utmost support, only wanting that I would dig deep and do my very best to achieve the thing that I was telling her I wanted."

Bradford's face had changed in these last few minutes of my recitation. He no longer wore an expression of deep grief and concern. Now he wore an expression of understanding, the light in his eyes showing that he knew what he was looking at, had seen it plenty before, and did not find my condition to be particularly alarming.

"So if you gave yourself 100 percent to your company and came home at the end of each day with real satisfaction in the work you did, Pam would be happy with her circumstances." Bradford wasn't asking a question. He was testing his understanding.

I nodded my head.

"And, alternatively, if you were to decide to go to work with me and then really got to work, making it a priority, doing what it takes to be successful, and sticking to it with determination and resolve, Pam would be supportive of you."

I nodded a second time.

"Do you have any idea how crazy lucky you are, Bobby?" Bradford then asked, a big smile on his face and an earnestness in the entirety of his expression. "You're married to a good woman, Bobby! She wants to back you and support you and be in your corner. All she's asking you to do is pick a wall where you're going to prop your ladder and then truly climb it! Make the commitment!"

I stared down at the floor. Bradford had pinpointed it. Pam was not waning in her support of me. I wasn't giving her anything to support.

"I get why she needs some time," I said, my eyes back off the floor and looking at my old work buddy. "And I'm good with her having some time with her folks and my kids being able to enjoy the incredible extended-family embrace that they get nowhere else on earth." I shook my head. "But I truly don't want to take this car back to Detroit and fly to that miserably empty property we call our home in Dallas," I added.

"You *have* to be in Dallas this next week?" The shrug of Bradford's shoulders suggested he was just wondering. Call him Colombo.

I most certainly did not need to be in Dallas the next week. It was a week of sales calls—by which I mean, literally, calls—and I'd be making those calls from my basement office of my Dallas home. Honestly, I could make them from the men's room at the airport.

"It's just a week of sales calls. What I need is my cell phone, not my city."

"Tell you what, Bobby," Bradford then said, instantly sitting half a foot taller. "My money's on Pam having no intention of getting rid of you." He was nodding his head in stone cold conviction. "She wants you to sort yourself out, and I don't know a woman worth her salt who isn't exactly like her where it comes to the man in her life."

I took his words in. I didn't have anything to say on the subject at that time.

"So the question is what do you want to do?"

That was it! He didn't elaborate but simply posed the question in its most elementary form. What do I want to do?

"I'd like to see your business, Bradford," I answered. "You could not be more correct that Pam is ready to stand behind me in my pursuits. She's perfectly happy being a corporate executive's wife, and she'd be happy not being one. The problem is I'm not happy being a corporate guy anymore—not in the least. There's something in me that wants to have my own business, to take a shot at my own venture. But the cost of starting a franchise or a conventional business is mind boggling to me, and I continue to run into the same dead end: lack of time and investment dollars."

"May I suggest a plan?" Bradford then said, seeing my amenability. "Stay here with us. The guesthouse above the garage is nicer than anyone deserves. It's got wireless and a little business center and is completely equipped for you to open up shop and take care of your work responsibilities this week. Stay there!" he continued, his entire being passionate about what he was saying. "I'm sure Chrissie would love to drive down to Pam's folks' house and check in with her, Bobby. They were buddies long ago, as you know, and she can have a girl-to-girl talk with Pam. And if I know Chrissie, she'll help you out a lot. And you and I can take a few hours to talk business."

I just stared at Bradford, and he gave me a couple of heartbeats.

"So you get to stick close by Pam and your kids. You take care of your business obligations and make those calls you need to make. Chrissie reaches out to Pam and helps bring some oxygen back into everybody's lungs. And I take a couple of hours to discuss what it would take to hit a long ball in my company. I'll sugarcoat nothing, disclose everything, and provide the real facts to allow you to make an intelligent and open-eyed assessment of how we're bringing value to the world. Our whole operating philosophy can be summed up in a quote attributed to Albert Einstein: 'The significant problems we face in life cannot be solved at the same level of thinking that created them.'[1] In other words, a person cannot change his life until he changes the way he thinks about the challenges in his life."

I remained quiet, continuing to hold eye contact. I was both very excited by what Bradford was proposing and terrified that my excitement would wither, as it had so many times before, leaving me demonstrating a most lackluster follow-through to his offer.

What I was thinking was, "That's exactly what I want, but I'm not sure whether I really want it." But how does one say such a thing or even admit to it?

"Let's do it!" That's what I actually said. I didn't want to go back to Dallas. I wanted to stay close to Pam. And I didn't want my career trajectory to continue on its current path, even though I did have some serious reservations about whether I would want anything to do with what Bradford would be showing me.

"Sounds great, Bobby! Let's do it! We'll get you settled here for tonight, and you and I will start out tomorrow morning and spend our first couple of hours together. Is that a deal?"

I nodded my head. "That's a deal!"

CHAPTER 4

ACTION STEP 1: GET ON THE TRAIN

I had forgotten to pack my suitcase. I knew this feeling intimately. I have had this same panicked sensation time after time, always too late, as I realized that my plans were being thwarted and that I might be out of time.

I looked around the room I was in and saw clothes strewn across the floor, most of them looking dirty. There was no suitcase in sight.

I clutched at my left-hand jacket pocket, remembering to double check that I had the ticket, and my panic ratcheted up even further. No ticket there. I tried the right-hand pocket, and found it empty, too. Where was it? I printed it, didn't I? The train was going to leave when? In minutes! And I didn't even have my ticket?

"We have to go!" I shouted. "Is everybody ready?" I shouted even louder. There was no reply, and then it dawned on me that my family might have left without me.

Dashing out the doorway of my bedroom, I opened door after door down the long hall in what I knew to be my house but appeared to be more like an endless dormitory hallway of bedroom after bedroom. Every room was empty. I opened a door, saw a stripped bed and clean-swept room, and ran to the next one, just to have the scene repeat itself again and again.

At the end of the hall, finally, I opened the last door and saw nothing in the room but a single piece of paper lying on the floor. With trepidation, I picked it up and read its few spare lines: "Hope you can make it, honey! We're heading to the train. Honestly, we just couldn't wait any longer! Pam."

I ran back down the hallway, this time searching for the room where I had started. Where were my clothes? I had minutes to get to the train station, couldn't find my ticket, and now didn't even know where the room was that had the clothes I would need to pack. In one final lunge with my hand, I swept open a doorway and heard a crash and thud, the whole scene suddenly plunging into utter darkness.

I could feel that I was lying in a bed. The darkness was total. It dawned on me that I had maybe knocked something off the bed stand to the left of me, but I couldn't picture exactly what I ordinarily kept there. I stretched my arm to the right to locate Pam, but instead of reaching into the aura of her warmth and finding the beloved human form that produced that warmth, my fingertips slid right across the expanse of cold sheet until they lipped over the right-hand edge of the bed.

I remembered then where I was.

Fumbling around the bed stand that I had just taken a swing at, I located my cell phone, pressed the on button, and saw that it was 3:00 a.m. Not a promising sign! A light sleeper by nature, my experience has always been that the hour I wake up is the hour my night is over. My hundred-miles-an-hour brain would turn the few hours that separated me from dawn into pure hell.

So I swung my legs over the side of the bed, waved my cell phone around the room for a second to catch sight of the room's light switch, and set about the task of starting my day.

Ten minutes later, I had a fresh cup of coffee in my hands, the room smelled of roast coffee deliciousness, I was in a pair of jeans and a T-shirt, and this journal was open in front of me, turned to a clean page.

"I've tried for a decade, without success, to talk myself into being satisfied with my job," I wrote.

"The best predictor of future behavior is past behavior." I had read this somewhere and wrote it down.

"Odds are, then, that I'm never going to be happy with my job."

"I've tried on prior occasions to launch a business of my own and almost immediately started sabotaging my success. I've never followed through on these opportunities by doing the things that success demands," I wrote.

"If the best predictor of future behavior is past behavior, does this mean that I'll also fail in Bradford's business?" That was my real question, and I needed this early morning hour to think this through. Wasn't this exactly what my dream was about, that I'd sabotage myself once again and lose the things that mattered to me most of all?

"So is anything different now?" That seemed like the important question to ask.

"I'm an idiot!" That's the response I wrote. "No, the fact that I'm an idiot isn't what's different. I'm an idiot, as in, of course something's different now!

"Pam has drawn a line. The stakes have just been ratcheted up by about 10,000 percent!" I nodded my head as I wrote this down. My dream about missing out on my family's trip on the train was horrible, and my reality in the wide-awake world was worse. I didn't want to lose Pam and the kids. I couldn't. I wouldn't!

"Is it true that the best predictor of what I'll do next is what I did in the past?" I wrote. "Does this formula always hold true?

"No!" I wrote this little word down with such a strong press on my paper that my pen nearly punctured the page. "The best predictor of my future is **NOT** my past behavior! The best predictor of my future behavior is what I think about myself, my past, and my future. Only when I change my thinking will I change my actions and results. This is what Pam has been trying to tell me. In fact, Bradford said pretty much the same thing yesterday with his Einstein quote. My thinking must change if I want my life to change!"

I stared at my journal. I recalled my uncertainty the day before when I declared to Bradford, "Let's do it!" I replayed the horrible scene in my dream and felt the panic of it coursing again through my body.

Then I wrote, "I've never lived through this day before. This is an entirely new kind of day, one unlike any other day in my entire life. The stakes are entirely new. 'A' doesn't equal 'B' any longer. It's time to get the old defeatist thoughts out of my brain and replace them with winning thoughts. As to what I will do with this new moment in my life, all bets are off! Why? Because it's time for me to think for a change!"

That was what I needed to get clear. I wasn't looking for any guarantees about what would happen next. I needed, rather, to throw off the voices of the tormentors, to evict the jeering "you're screwed" hecklers that lived in my brain like they owned the joint. Who knew what I would do next? I certainly didn't! I've never been in this spot before, and the stakes have never been so utterly extreme.

With this point clear — all bets are off! — I felt encouraged and fortified. "Let's do it!" I then wrote, noting that my head and my heart were, this time, in far greater accord. It occurred to me that Pam was loving me even still, her line in the sand offering me what could, ultimately, be the greatest gift she had ever offered.

I remembered a poster I read once. It said, "If you don't like the results you've produced in life, perhaps it's time to stop taking your own advice!" Indeed! I didn't like the results, and I was taking in new advice. With tears in my eyes, I said a little prayer for Pam, and I felt thankful, my wretched situation notwithstanding.

And then, I got myself a second cup of coffee and began to make a list of the questions that I wanted to ask Bradford when we met later in the morning.

When Bradford and I sat down to breakfast (Chrissie had whipped up a couple of amazing omelets, plus bacon, more coffee, and orange juice), I felt ready — not in the sense of having no qualms about what I was about to embark upon, but ready to ask my questions. I'm an engineer, after all. I've got to understand how the machine works. I ordinarily read the spec sheets before I buy anything, and this wasn't an ordinary "purchase." Pam deserved my utmost, from my due diligence on this venture to my faithful execution of 100 percent of the disciplines and behaviors that success would require of me.

As I had just made crystal clear to myself, I had never been in this situation before. My loving wife had raised the stakes, and all my chips were now sitting squarely in the middle of the table. And my heart and will for excellence had become a flaming torch.

"Overnight, I thought about where I need to start with my questions this morning, Bradford," I began, "and I've gotten really clear."

Bradford remained quiet. I had his full attention. The impression I got was that he was not only *not* trying to sell me something, but that I was perhaps more on the hot seat than he was. I felt like a student about to sit for an exam, and I wondered, by the stillness and expectancy of Bradford, if my first question — the question that I had selected to ask first — was my first test.

"I'm sure you start out with someone like me by showing them the business plan. But if you don't mind, I'd like to start at a more fundamental place. I'm not a first-timer to network marketing, and I'll understand the plan well when we get to it. But can we talk a little bit about business itself — about how you understand what makes a business a good business?"

"The metaphysics of our business, as it were," Bradford clarified. "You bet! Fire away!"

"Does your company provide real value to the marketplace?"

The barest bend of a smile bloomed on Bradford's face, and I swear that it was followed by a hint of moistness in his eyes.

"I mean," I stammered on, "is there a legitimate product involved? And do we offer it at a competitive price that gives us — and the people who join us — a real chance to make real sales?" There was passion in my question. This mattered to me first and foremost. And there was also insecurity in my heart. Would my first question be the end of our meeting?

Bradford took a big, cleansing breath. He shook his head and allowed his spare smile to spread. "Bobby, you just made my day! No, my month! One of the principles we teach is to keep the main thing the main thing, and the main thing in our business is to satisfy our customers by providing value into their lives."

I couldn't help but feel good that Bradford recognized my desire to study his business honestly and thoroughly.

"The job of a business, Bobby, is to bring value to the world. Network marketing brings value to the world through simplifying the marketing of products and services. For instance, according to Nielsen, 92 percent of consumers believe recommendations from friends and family over all other forms of advertising.[1] Network marketing is simply word-of-mouth advertising at its finest. Remember, if the business doesn't bring value to the world, doesn't serve the world by doing things, building things, and serving its customers in valuable ways, at prices they can afford, there is never a reason to consider point two!" Bradford was clearly as passionate on the subject as I was.

"But you said your company has been accused of being a pyramid," I said. "Every pyramid I've seen makes a product that's just window dressing, and the real game is recruiting distributors. Nothing ever gets retailed because the product isn't the point, and it's too expensive anyway. You might be successful at recruiting new distributors, but those new distributors couldn't sell the product if their life depended on it. So they focus all *their* effort on recruiting still *more* distributors!"

"*Accused* of being a pyramid is what I said, Bobby!" Bradford countered. "All network marketing companies are accused of being pyramids because few understand the difference between a legitimate network marketing company and an illegal pyramid. I wouldn't be caught dead associated with a pyramid scheme! A person's character is everything in life and leadership."

"So there is a legitimate product?"

"Our product is my entire reason for being in business, Bobby. Our leadership products change the way people think and act and, thus, the results they produce in life. In fact, our bestselling product is the *Financial Fitness Pack*, which has helped thousands of customers eliminate debt and live free from financial stress.

"Network marketing companies pay volume rebates to members who generate business volume for them. For example, if a new car I want costs $35,000, do you think the dealership would offer a discount if I told them I had twenty-five friends in a car club who wanted the same car? Of course, the dealership would offer a discount, and no one would accuse them of being a pyramid for doing so. Volume discounts are a way of life in conventional business, and network marketing has created an entire business model around the concept.

"Let me give you my first rule on sizing up a business opportunity: If the company pays you commissions purely on recruiting others to be in the company — never on reaching customers with a great product — walk away immediately! The facts are, Bobby," he pressed on, "that over $167 billion worth of merchandise is sold each year worldwide through network marketing, and its true potential is still untapped. In my experience, I have found that the confusion between a legitimate network marketing company and an illegitimate pyramid scheme has actually been helpful. The best leaders in different fields are just starting to awaken to the opportunities available in lawful network marketing companies. The ignorance in the marketplace, then, is an opportunity for those who are willing to lead and educate.

"The key difference between network marketing and a pyramid scheme, for example," Bradford continued, "is that in a pyramid scheme, the person who gets in first makes more than those who get in later. The payouts are based merely on chronological hierarchy and not performance. In contrast, a person's income in a viable network marketing company isn't based upon his chronological position but rather his performance. Top performers, in other words, quickly pass their sponsors in income and rank even though their sponsors joined first. Our company, LIFE Leadership, rewards results: actual volume moved to the community and its customers. You could sponsor a person who goes on to make millions of dollars through building several compensated communities, while you only make a few hundred dollars because you didn't. Why? These two factors—actual customer sales and pay for performance rather than positions—differentiate a legal network marketing company from an illegal pyramid."

My brain went, "Check!" I couldn't have agreed more with Bradford's first rule. An "opportunity" that doesn't come with a sacred duty to serve a customer—to do something of true value and to do it at a competitive price—is nothing less than a get-rich-quick scheme. A fraud. A scam, a sham, and a blight. I believe this to the bottom of my shoes. And I did know that there was a huge volume of customer business going on within the network marketing profession.

"You just talked about someone making millions of dollars," I said. "Do people get rich quick in your company?" It wasn't on my list to ask, but our conversation brought me to the question.

Bradford nodded approvingly at the question, "Some work their businesses diligently, doing everything that success demands, putting in the hours, and defeating their doubts and fears. And those who do are able to make a great living! I fell in love with network marketing because I realized quickly that your pay raise becomes effective as soon as you do, and no internal politics can stop you from advancing as far and as fast as you desire. However, not everyone gets wealthy, Bobby. In truth, most people joining our company aren't seeking wealth at all. They join to improve themselves and associate with an encouraging community. Our company is less about getting rich, whether fast or slow, and more about making a difference. We do that by providing life-changing information to individuals, communities, and companies. And since everything rises and falls on leadership, we contribute value to the world by teaching our customers and members how to raise their leadership game, whatever their chosen profession or business is.

"Bobby, you and I both worked in a large corporation where they stack their executives, managers, and staff into a tightly hierarchical pyramid. It didn't take us long to realize that we could not advance unless someone exited the organization through retirement, demotion, transfer, or termination. This automatically makes the climb to the top slow regardless of how fast one is growing and changing. When I was in the corporate world, I felt like I was driving behind a slow car without being permitted to pass. LIFE Leadership is different. We directly reward diligence, drive, and mastery with more income and recognition as you build your own business. True wealth, then, results from consistently amazing your customers and members, who then share their experiences with others.

"So if it sounds too good to be true, Bobby, it probably is. That's point number two."

I nodded. I liked what I was hearing so far. One: there was true value creation (any enduring business is anchored to delivering value). Two: vision and diligence were key (true success *always* pivots on these two). And three: there were real rewards (as there must be if what is offered is actually valuable).

"All my initial questions are about your business principles," I said. It had suddenly occurred to me to just lay my cards on the table. I wanted to know what governed company decisions. Honestly, I don't first and foremost care what the company sells or how much money they promise to pay, not if they're going to conduct themselves in ways I'd find embarrassing.

"So, that being the case," I pressed on, "why don't you just tell me what the difference is between the truly great network marketing companies and the many hyped-up, fly-by-night varieties that are here today and gone tomorrow?" If Bradford hadn't been so disarmingly candid—and clear-eyed—on my first questions, I might have gone right on playing cat and mouse with him. But he'd gained miles of trust with me in the first few feet of our conversation, and I was ready to speed up this get-acquainted session!

Bradford smiled—really smiled. "Love it!" was his whole preamble. And then he launched.

"So let's call this point three: be wary of hype and the famous 'ground floor opportunity.' Although some people might claim you earn more money if you get in first, this is *never, ever* the case in a legitimate network marketing company. Actually, Bobby," he continued, "if they say you have to get in first, chances are much greater that they'll fold within the first couple of years. It is much safer to join a company with a proven track record."

Bradford didn't know it, but I wholeheartedly agreed from personal experience!

"Point four I already just stated: Does the company have a proven track record? The Chairman of the Board, Orrin Woodward, and the CEO, Chris Brady, of LIFE Leadership were both included in *Inc.* magazine's May 2014 list of the Top 50 Leadership and Management Experts in the world. These two *New York Times* bestselling leadership authors were the masterminds behind LIFE Leadership and were the only leaders on the *Inc.* magazine list from the *same* company."

Bradford was beaming as he discussed his good friends and business partners. "But more important, I know these leaders personally as well as the other founders and LIFE Coaches I have spoken with at conventions around the country. I have studied their leadership and entrepreneurship firsthand for the past ten years and consider it one of my greatest privileges to work with the other LIFE Coaches in the Policy Council meetings. These get-togethers ensure the corporate and field leaders are aligned in vision, purpose, and practices."

Bradford was on a roll, answering questions before I had even formulated them. He continued, "And since every company rises and falls on its leadership, I chose to work with proven leaders rather than chase the latest hyped-up product. I learned a long time ago that companies based on hyped-up products come and go, but the enduring companies succeed through great leadership."

"I know that's true from my own experiences," I interrupted. "I joined several companies with hyped-up products but little leadership. Why don't more companies focus on leadership?"

"Why?" Bradford paused. "Because real leadership takes time and effort to change people from the inside out, but a super product claims to change people overnight and with ease from the outside in. People fall for the something-for-nothing hype even though they know the best things in life take time, focus, and energy. Great leaders know that people are their greatest resource and create learning cultures for people to grow and change. Poor leaders, in contrast, believe a super product is the secret and therefore make no effort to build a learning culture. Thus, when the organization reaches its leadership lid, the company falls as quickly as it rose."

Bradford clearly was a professional who had invested the time to know his profession. I was not shocked he had reached the top in the network marketing field. Then he said, "One more thought: I like working with a company that has a proven track record because the longer it has been in business, the better chance the governing bodies are aware of the business model. Pyramid schemes, in other words, simply do not last long in the marketplace."

Bradford could have stopped here, as far as I was concerned. My head was nodding up and down like a bobblehead. This man was cut from the very same cloth of integrity and business virtue that I was. We'd gone far enough down this road that I was confident I knew everything else that made him tick from a business principles standpoint.

But Bradford wasn't finished, and his face radiated enthusiasm and joy for this subject. "Point five, Bobby, is that the company needs to be absolutely clear that they'll buy back any unsold product(s). Most network marketing companies—and this company falls under the umbrella of a network marketing company—have a thirty-day, no-questions-asked, money-back guarantee, which means that if you are unhappy with the products, all you have to do is send them back for a refund. In our case, customers and members can get a full refund for any products returned within the first thirty days. Everything is refunded, including the cost of the business starter kit, no questions asked, within thirty days of purchasing."

Bradford grinned. The boyishness and enthusiasm he felt toward his company was on full display. I liked this! There's nothing like a leader who loves what he does and who truly and absolutely believes in his company! Money cannot buy what this is worth to the success of an enterprise and to the success of the people who give their lives to that business.

"It's like this, Bobby," Bradford continued. This man was on a roll. He was literally sitting on the edge of his seat, and his hands were flying as he gesticulated and underscored his points. "Try LIFE Leadership, do a great job, and you may achieve your dreams, or at a minimum, you will become better through applying wisdom to life's challenges." He gave a thumbs-up with his right hand to punctuate this point. "Or if you find that it isn't for you," the thumb was up on his left hand now, "you can get a refund on anything purchased within the last thirty days, no questions asked. As Stephen Covey liked to say, it's a 'Win/Win or No Deal'![2]

"Two more, Bobby," he went on. "Point six: benchmark the best! If you're looking into network marketing for the first time, don't be scared to look at other business models and products, particularly if you don't know which company to join. Being an engineer, I studied the various models, methods, and marketing plans for network marketing. I invested the time and money to understand what made the best the best so that I could be part of the best leadership community that delivers a world-class product with a world-class compensation plan. I know that you will see the difference right away, since you've had previous experience with network marketing.

"And point seven: make sure they train exceptionally well. I'll get to this point next time we meet, but it does you no good whatsoever to figure out by yourself how to do this business. You might be a quick study or just naturally talented, but that's not enough. You've got to have all the confidence in the world that there's a training system in place for the people you're trying to help. You want everybody to have a chance to be great, not just the exceptional person here or there, and that means great training is key! The company you join has to have a fantastic training system, one *you* can lean on and one that you can recommend to *everybody* who joins you.

"How's that, for starters?" Bradford knew that he had just given me the fire-hydrant version of Business Principles 101, and he was grinning. He also knew that I had grasped the essence; our principles aligned.

"So what do I do next?"

"Tell me where you want to go, and I will help you get on the right train to get there. It's your call, Bobby! There's a lot I can do to help you, but the thing I can't do is tell you what it is that you want to do.

"What do you want to do?" he asked again as he had the day before.

"Well...I want to win. And, honestly, I like my chances of winning better if I am working with you. For starters, I would like a business and a life like yours, Bradford!" That was what I wanted, and it felt great to have that clear. "I'm in! So what's the first thing I should do?"

"Get yourself a seat on this train! Hold your spot! Everything else you will need to learn, you'll learn on the journey.

"Now that we are partners, let me add one more thing," he continued. Bradford's face was as resolute as a smelter in a steel mill. "As my partner, I will never, ever quit on you! You might quit on me, but you can take it to the bank that I will never quit on you. I treat my business partners with the same level of commitment I made to Chrissie — for better or for worse."

I loved it. Bradford's way of thinking made quitting not an option. This is the kind of new thinking I was taking into my own life—new thinking that would lead to new behavior.

"Did you just call this company a '*train*'?" I then asked, my face surely looking amazed.

He nodded.

"I had a nightmare last night," I explained. "Pam and the kids left me behind and were headed to catch a train. I was scrambling like mad to get packed so I could catch the train before it left, but I knew I wouldn't make it."

We just stared at each other. Bradford was shaking his head in wonder.

"And you say, 'Get yourself a seat on this train!'"

"Coincidences are just God's way of remaining anonymous, Bobby. That dream wasn't random." He leaned forward. "I always use the metaphor of a train in helping people understand what it takes to be successful in this profession. And my <u>Action Step 1</u> is always: <u>Get On the Train</u>! You want to get started? That's how you start!"

"I need to get moving, Bradford," I responded. "I have procrastinated long enough. I can learn as we go. With your help, I'll figure this game out as I play it."

Bradford was really smiling. He knew, as I knew, that great leaders have a bias for action. Nothing wins like initiative. Some people say, "Ready!...Aim!...Fire!" I like Tom Peters' version: "Fire! Fire! Fire!"[3] I had a lot more questions, but I knew I would improve my aim by shooting. "Implementation...," Peters says, "[is] the 'last 98 percent' of the client puzzle."[4]

"Sign me up, Bradford," I said. "Get me on the train. The best way for me to learn is to get to work."

"We'll do it right now, Bobby, and we'll get you straight to work," he responded, "but there's one more, absolutely vital and critical thing."

He had my full attention.

"You'll hear me say this again and again. You have to start right now to get your mind and heart prepared to live and lead at a new level. I can't pour new ideas into an old Bobby Davis. If I do, you'll just leak! We've got to grow your capacity to receive and hold the new things—the true things—that you must learn and act upon if you're going to produce new results in life.

"And I'm not going to be able to travel around with you 24–7 to keep reinforcing these things; you have to do this work continuously to grow your mind and heart to be able to learn the principles needed for success in every area of life."

Bradford's face was warm, but stern. I was getting the most intense part of his instructions right here, and I just waited to hear how I would actually do what he was telling me was vital to do.

"I'll introduce you next time to the system we use for all of this—it's called Club 180°—but until then, here's a starter pack of books and audios. Read! Listen! And associate! There is so much you already do right, Bobby, and the books and audios will fuel you to drive out the remaining false messages and lies holding you back from seizing your future. Read at least thirty minutes every day and listen to three audios every day from the men and women who've broken through and can teach you how to do it! We'll provide great books and audios for you. Also, we'll get you plugged into your local Open Meeting and Monthly Seminar in the Dallas area to associate with other leaders growing there.

"The books you read, the audios you listen to, and the people you associate with, Bobby—those are the difference makers! If you want to really be a go-getter, make this a daily priority! And I'll teach you how to emphasize this throughout your team."

I needed no further urging. My thought was, "If Bradford says that this is vital to my success and that I should do it, then I'm gonna do it!"

We had finished our omelets, talked through all the preliminary questions, and Bradford had gotten me signed up, securing my position on his team. We had talked about some of the next-step details and brewed a new pot of coffee. The first steps were done, and we had just settled back into the recliners with fresh cups of coffee. "Chrissie gave Pam a call early this morning, Bobby," Bradford said.

I had figured that the important part of my day was done and expected to go back to my flat above Bradford's garage and begin my week of corporate sales calls. I wasn't looking forward to the duty I still had to serve.

But Bradford's remark instantly electrified me. I hadn't anticipated this development. True, he had told me the night before that Chrissie would reach out to Pam. They were, after all, friends in their teenage years. And I knew that Bradford and Chrissie were people of action. Still, it took me by surprise that Chrissie had moved so quickly and that she had already been successful in getting Pam on the phone.

"How'd it go?"

It was such a small question, but my heart was beating like the Big Bertha drum the Texas Longhorns use in Austin.

"You're a very fortunate, dude, Bobby," Bradford began, his face sober. "Pam loves you a lot." He paused, choosing his words carefully. "The short of it is that she needs something new out of you, which I know that you already know." His voice had softened. This last statement—which, on the face of it, could have been construed as harsh—was made with the utmost of kindness.

I breathed in and realized that I had been holding my breath. My heart flooded with gratitude, and to my consternation, I felt my eyes brim with tears, which I promptly blinked clear—or tried to. I nodded my head.

"She has every right to need and expect something new out of me," I stated, not particularly aiming my comment back at Bradford. She did! She had every right! I was affirming a truth to myself—and to the universe.

"How did she greet the news of my new scheme? No offense, Bradford," I quickly added. "I just assume anything I do next is going to strike her as a scheme."

Bradford smiled. There was no trace of offense taken. He shrugged. "Chrissie didn't report on that part. I know she told Pam what you and I are discussing, but I don't get the impression that Pam is worried about what it is, particularly, that you're going to do next."

I nodded my head again. That made sense. "She's worried about *how* I'm going to do what I do—how I'm going to follow through—and if I'm going to put my head down and get the job done or take quick action and then flinch, start complaining, and begin the back-pedaling she's seen before."

Bradford said not a word. I knew that he shared my analysis precisely. What was there to say?

"Okay." It was, indeed, okay. "Better than okay," I added, taking another big breath. It was, in point of fact, way better than okay. Pam was taking nothing from me. Far fairer to say, Pam was giving me everything. The ball was in my court, and I had the strongest sense that she was still—perhaps now more than ever—my greatest cheerleader on earth. She was *for* me, for *us*, and she was showing it in the way that gave me the absolute best chance of becoming what I most longed to become, both for myself and for her and our family.

It was time to get to work!

CHAPTER 5

ACTION STEP 2: GET OTHERS ONTO THE TRAIN

"Bob, I don't know what else I can tell you. Pam is aware of your outreach, and it's not that she doesn't appreciate it. But my instructions are to hold her calls. She's decided, for the time being, to be offline, which is why I'm keeping her cell phone."

I made no reply. The phone went very quiet as I contemplated, again, Pam's unwillingness to answer my calls. I had no retort, no reply, no words.

"You know I love you, Bob!"

My father-in-law's voice had suddenly become very scratchy, and the strong, wall-built-high voice that he had started with when he answered—this was my third call to my wife's mobile number in the span of several hours—was now a shadow of itself. I knew that he did love me. I knew that he was terribly pained by what was going on. And I knew, from the years I've spent with this good man, that he'd go to great lengths to ease my pain if he could. Phil DeVries is the most kind and conciliatory human being I have ever known, but at that moment, he was taking a completely one-sided stand.

On my prior call, my father-in-law had put each of my kids on the line. From what I could tell, they were having a wonderful time. I know Pam, and I am confident that she isn't dragging our children into this difficult time in our marriage. I heard their tales of wonder from their various escapades as they "played" — which on the DeVries' farm, means "worked" — with their cousins in the barn and the garden. Mostly I heard animal stories, and I was cheered by their joy and enthusiasm. For my kids, this was a normal week; that is to say, the part of this week that involved my absence was normal. Their dad was, as per usual, somewhere other than where they were, which was par for their course.

But after hanging the phone up, my desire to hear Pam's voice — it felt like a need — took over again, and in due course, I called yet another time.

"Pam has asked me to hold her calls, Bob. She wants some time to reflect and pray and listen to her soul," Phil said, "and I'm going to honor that request." He cleared his throat. "She has her reasons," he added, a deep pain in his voice as he reminded me of a fact that I knew all too well. Phil's grief practically bled across the airwaves, traversing the distance that separated us and seeping right into my handset.

She has her reasons. Of course she has her reasons. And I respected what she was doing completely. But I still wanted to talk to my wife!

"Would you give her a message, Dad?" I managed to ask, my voice forced through a great pressure in my throat.

"Of course, Son," my father-in-law answered, his voice smaller still.

"Tell Pam I'm heading out now. I'll be in Dallas the rest of the week."

Another silence filled the line.

"And give her my love," I then added. I wanted to say more — to lash out, to be honest — but I managed to contain myself.

"You bet," was all this "man's man" had left to say. You bet!

And I *was* betting! I was betting my life!

Bradford and I had met for a second time earlier that morning — Tuesday — to pick up where we had left off on Monday. When we had wrapped up our work, it was past lunchtime, and I knew that the only way to begin taking action on what I'd learned in my second day of apprenticeship under my old friend was to go home to Dallas, home to where I had many networks and acquaintances, and get straight to work. Bradford agreed with my thinking about this, so I had found an early evening flight out of Detroit, packed my bags, and finished the drive to the airport that I had begun two days earlier — a lifetime ago, it felt — back on Sunday morning.

It was while I was packing up my things that I had called Pam for the first time, and on that first call, I had only spoken briefly with Phil. I felt mesmerized, as I zipped up my bags, by the realization that, this time, there was no nightmarish panic. My paperless e-ticket was right there in my smartphone, tucked into my sports coat, where I had put it after I did my online check-in. There was no rushing down an endless hallway, no throwing open door after door, panicked that my family might have gone without me. In truth, they *had* gone without me, but unlike my nightmare from Sunday night, I had been completely calm as I packed. Yes, I was about to fly away *from* them, but I knew that this was the pathway back *to* them, and as pained as I was, I was also at peace.

In the car, driving south to the Detroit Metropolitan Wayne County Airport, I had called Pam for the second time, and it was during that second call that Phil had put my children on the line so that I could speak with each one.

And sitting at my gate is where I completed my third call, asking my father-in-law to tell my precious Pam that I loved her.

My flight was on a posted twenty-minute delay — which was not untypical for a DFW–bound route — and I figured that, if all went well, the boarding call would still be a good forty minutes off. I wondered if anybody sitting around me had eavesdropped on my phone call with my father-in-law. It struck me that listening in to my side of that call could have led others to a very wrong conclusion about the "tragedy" that was unfolding in my life.

I had pleaded with my father-in-law to put my wife on the phone—and not quietly—and anybody with a brain would have deduced that I'd failed in my effort. This must have seemed very pathetic to the people sitting kneecap to kneecap with me.

But I didn't feel pathetic. And I didn't believe for a second that I was in the middle of a tragedy. With a certainty that I don't think I can adequately explain, I firmly believed that my wife was doing what she was doing because she was *for* me—because she *hadn't* abandoned me. She was keeping me on the raw edge of a vitally necessary hunger, refusing to offer me, too early, an easing of my need, of my drive, of my mind, of my will. Pam had watched me closely over the years and seen my underperformance each time I had moved from a second-in-command position to first-in-command—a move that every business owner has to make. And in times past, she had seen me flinch, duck for cover, look for comfort, need to talk, and start making excuses.

This was the very first time in my life that I was, real deal, first-in-command, and my gut told me that Pam knew, at least intuitively, that I needed to remain wide awake to just how weighty my duty was.

I would have put money on this declaration that I felt in my gut: "But for her extreme love for me and her devotion to do whatever it takes to cooperate with my success, Pam would be throwing herself into my arms right now just as ardently as I'd like to throw myself into hers. She needs my comfort just as desperately as I need hers. But she's tough! And she's going for something that's far more important than comfort. She's going for transformation—mine, hers, and ours."

Pam knew that I was taking a new kind of step into manhood, that is, a new step into adulthood, not a chronological step into manhood but a responsibility step. I passed the age of twenty-one nearly two decades ago, but I've never become a no-excuses man, an "if it is to be, then it is up to me" man.

And it was high time.

And knowing this—believing this—caused me to see that Pam was paying as dear a price as I was, perhaps even greater.

Whatever the passengers sitting around me might have been thinking about my situation, what I was thinking was, "Bradford Henderson is right! I am one very fortunate dude!" I was thinking that, but at the very same time, I was feeling like pure hell.

I took a deep breath and then pulled out my notes from the morning. It was time to get it all down clearly on paper so that my plans would be ready for what I needed to do when I hit the ground in Dallas.

"Yesterday we covered <u>Action Step 1: Get On the Train</u>." That's where Bradford had begun earlier in the morning. We had met in his planning room, and he'd pulled out several whiteboards to help him with his teaching session. "Today, Bobby, is <u>Action Step 2: Get Others onto the Train</u>. You've held your spot on the train, and now it's time to start helping others join you."

"May I interrupt you right there," I had interjected. I hadn't planned to bring such early objections, but one had immediately leapt to mind.

"Go!"

"A lot of people who join a network marketing company never actually get themselves going. They get talked into it, or they join with a hope to get somewhere new in their lives, and then they just sit there." I said it, but I wasn't sure yet what my question was.

Bradford waited.

"So is it a screening problem?" I ventured. It occurred to me that this might be the answer to my own question. "Is there a better way to determine who will be successful and then just recruit the ones who are truly ready and able?"

Still, Bradford waited.

"Or," I lurched onward, "is it a support problem? You talked yesterday about training and about how important a good training system is. Is it a training problem?"

Bradford's head nodded once. The gesture indicated to me that he was satisfied with my question. Or perhaps it's better to say that he was satisfied with the way that I had rolled up my sleeves and become engaged with my own question. Or perhaps better yet to say that he was satisfied to see that the reason I was asking my question was not to be a naysayer or a spitballer but rather to be a problem solver. I was looking for actual answers, which made my question genuine and not a dodge.

"Good, Bobby!" he began earnestly. "I like the way you think! Let's unpack that question." He got up, picked up a dry-erase marker, and started writing on one of his white boards.

"For a lot of people to be successful in a business like ours, three things must be present. 'Right Business' is the first one." He wrote, *"1. Right Business,"* on his board. "We talked about this yesterday. Does the company sell something that's worthwhile? Does the product or service compete in the marketplace? Are there customers who want it? Is the price right, is the quality excellent, and so forth?"

He turned to look at me. I was nodding. "I've got that one," I stated. Success begins with the "Right Business." Of course it does.

Bradford swung back around to his board. "Second," he continued, "is 'Right People.'" He wrote, *"2. Right People"* just under *"1. Right Business."* I nodded, copying into my journal what he was writing on the board.

"Are there leaders in my support team who will help my new people do the proper steps? Does the company train and empower its new people to know how to be successful within this business? Nothing sells itself, Bobby!" Bradford continued, his voice sharp. I could feel his passion—his anger, even—as he addressed just how important it is to give people everything they need to be able to be successful. "So 'Right People' means that new partners can be assured that they will have good leaders around them—leaders who help them become successful. And we are responsible for being those 'Right People' on behalf of the new members that we invite to join us. I need to be one of those 'good leaders' for you, Bobby, and you're going to need to learn how to be one for the people joining your community."

"And the training system is a part of this," I ventured. I was pretty sure I was getting this.

"Absolutely!" Bradford practically crowed. "When you bring someone in, Bobby, you're one of the 'Right People' I'm talking about. But the great thing is that you can lean on our excellent live meetings, audios, and books to help you develop your leadership personally and professionally. The best leaders produce content in our training system to teach, train, and inspire straight into the hearts and minds of the people you sponsor. We're all the 'Right People,' and the training system assures that new people learn from the best of the best right away."

"Yesterday, you had me make a commitment to immediately start reading and listening to audios to get the reinforcement I need for what I'm learning. This is what you're talking about."

"Exactly! Leverage is the key to great leadership. Look; you can learn 90 percent of what you need to learn to excellently run this company without me in the room. You can do it by reading great books, listening to great audios, and being disciplined about making this a priority every day. And as you bring people into the business, they can learn 90 percent of what they need to learn by doing the same thing. We've got to rely on the system here to grow ourselves and to grow our people because teaching

100 percent of everything to each person one-on-one is, quite frankly, impossible.

"What that allows then," Bradford said, very excited, "is for me to invest the time I can dedicate to you for that critical 10 percent of your learning that will help you get the highest-leverage results. This is the art side of the business, and if I have limited time for you, which I do, I want to spend our mentoring time on the crucial 10 percent that cannot be taught in a book or audio because it's personal to you. And you'll want to do this with your people in exactly the same way, teaching them to read the books and listen to the audios and using your time for the highest leverage possible to help them in their business building.

"Lean on the books, audios, and association. And teach your people to do the same thing. Make sense?"

I nodded. It did make sense, and I was tracking, for sure.

"But I haven't gotten to the heart of your question yet, so let me back up and address it," Bradford continued. "You asked if we should learn how to screen better so that we don't bring people in who won't or can't do the work. You pointed out that people can join a network marketing company completely dedicated to becoming successful and can end up not doing anything but just sitting—failing as a business person, in reality.

"True?" he pressed. "That was your question, wasn't it? How do we make sure that the people who join will actually succeed?"

True. That was my question.

"A lot of people who join a network marketing company never actually get themselves going," I repeated. "That was what I said. And I wondered if we can do something about this."

Bradford's nod of the head was so huge, so emphatic this time that he could have thrown a Sumo wrestler off his back with it.

"Love it!" he repeated. "Your question tells me you want just what I want and that you're pained by the very same things that pain me!"

I took in his remark, and I wondered if he was going to actually answer my question.

"I've got a question for *you*, Bobby," he then continued.

Fair enough.

"Are you, for sure—and I mean, for sure—going to do everything that success demands of you in my company?"

I just stared at him for a second.

"I am," I then answered. But I already knew where this was going.

"And tell me: How am I to know that what you just said is true? How does Bradford Henderson know that Bobby Davis is ready—*really* ready? Can you show me your certificate of guaranteed readiness?"

I smiled and, I suspect, blushed. I couldn't show him this. And hadn't I just grilled myself with this very same question? Why on earth should I believe I'm going to make this work, given my track record of not making it work before? And why should I be sitting smack-dab in the middle of the grand estate of one of the top leaders in the company, when all I could really tell him was that, well, I was pretty sure that I was ready to do better this time. And how did I know that I would do better this time? Well, just because, sir! Because this time was different! Really and truly, sir! This time, I would make it work! Not like the last time, sir. No, sir! And, for sure, not like the time before that or even the one before *that*. No siree! I was a brand-spankin'-new kind of guaranteed performer! Pretty sure of it, as a matter of fact, so far as I could tell!

The smile kept playing on the corners of my mouth. I had just been wondering about the irresponsibility of inviting people into a business who might not decide to do what success required. And at the same time, I was desperately and fervently hoping that I'd be allowed to join this company, even though I couldn't prove—not even if my life depended on it—that I'd do what success required. My track record—let's be honest here—stunk!

I just shook my head. I could not myself prove that I would do what success required. I could not, that is, until I actually *did* what success required. We'd have to give me a chance, and then we'd see.

Bradford had a smile on his face, too. He saw my mind working—and probably saw my heart getting fully wrapped around just how sacred this moment was. And then he walked back to his white board.

"*3. Right Time,*" he wrote.

"I don't know about you, Bobby, but I don't know who's ready to crush it. I've got some superstars—million-aires now—who had major obstacles to overcome when

I signed them up. And I've got some people who looked absolutely perfect on paper, and yet they won't do a single thing that success demands. They look great and talk the talk and know practically everybody on earth, but for reasons that they and they alone know, they aren't ready to walk the walk."

Bradford let his comment hang in the air.

"Some people say it's unfair to get people's hopes up. I guess they think since not everyone is going to do the work, you shouldn't talk to anyone." And it was right there in Bradford's commentary that, I swear, smoke started coming out of his ears. "I beg to differ. The real unfair thing, as far as I'm concerned, Bobby," he continued, his head practically igniting into a fireball, "is when there are human beings who are *ambitious*," (He smacked his points down into his left hand with his right-hand pointer finger outstretched, hammering down each of them like a blacksmith striking at a rod of molten iron.) "...*teachable*," (The hammer struck again, and the sparks flew.) "...*and looking for a good opportunity*," (Smack! Bradford paused, perhaps to catch his breath. And then his right arm reached back for one final blow.) "...*but no one is willing to introduce them to the right opportunity because everyone prejudged their chances of making it. Never forget, Bobby, that many times, success is camouflaged. And it's our responsibility to peel away the layers until the winner within is revealed to the world. I have witnessed radical changes in too many people's lives to ever surrender this point.*"

I didn't interrupt. I knew that I was getting a peek into the deep and fundamental motivation of this man. Bradford believed that all human beings deserved a chance. And he wasn't going to play God.

He took a breath and smiled. "In sum, Bobby, I would rather share this opportunity with everyone and let the cream rise to the top. I refuse to prejudge them; I refuse to play God in their lives; I just help them identify what they want and show them how to get it. Then they can decide what they want to do with the opportunity based on their hunger, timing, and options."

This made deep, moral sense to me. What? Was I a prophet? No! Was I a god? Did I have the skill or even the right, for that matter, to decide who would get a chance and who wouldn't? What did I know about such things?

"Bobby," Bradford continued, "we have a thirty-day, no-questions-asked return policy. And it's a ninety-nine-dollar sign-up fee! No one can be damaged financially by jumping into this company, which is absolutely *not* the case for people joining a conventional business venture."

"1. Right Business."

"2. Right People."

"3. Right Time."

That's what I had put down in my notes earlier in the morning. And getting that down was what led to my decision to fly back to Dallas. I knew it was my "Right Time." I didn't want Bradford Henderson, or anyone else, telling me whether I was ready this time. Getting that clear unlocked a floodgate of names of people I knew that might be ready to do something new with their lives.

My twenty-minute delay had turned into an hour delay, but that was a blessing. I wrapped up my notes, filled out a prospect list of 150 people I was going to reach out to, packed away my journal and pens, and boarded my flight.

Bradford had agreed to fly down to join me on Friday and Saturday. We were going to do my first presentations, and he was personally going to set the template for how it's done. So I had my work cut out for me. It was time to "Get Others onto the Train"!

CHAPTER 6

THE OPPORTUNITY

I know a lot of people. And my list of 150 people was daunting to me, as I had only two and a half days before Bradford would arrive. However, I vowed to reach out to as many as I could in order to take advantage of his visit.

Bradford had given me a way to think about the kind of person I should be looking for when he gave me his impassioned words: *Teachable*, *Ambitious*, and *Looking for a good opportunity*. But I needed some more help to cull down my list, so I gave him a quick ring Wednesday morning. I was going to hit the phones and also make a number of important face-to-face visits, and I wanted to prioritize my list as well as I could before jumping into it.

If at all possible, I would reach every one of them in my limited hours. But knowing people's lives as I do, I was aware that I'd be fighting my way through to reach everyone within the time I had. Nonetheless, Bradford

Henderson was coming to see me, and I wanted to be as strategic with this opportunity as possible.

"Bobby," Bradford barked. He wasn't being rude; it's just that he was as short on time as I was, and he wanted to pack as much as possible into the minute that he could spare. "Follow this rule of thumb as you decide the order of your calls. You want somebody who's ambitious; that's number one." I already had that one from the day before. "You want somebody who is looking for something more in life; that's number two." I had that one, too. He had given me "looking for a good opportunity" when I was with him. "You want somebody who is teachable; I can't stress that enough." Had that one, too. "And," he continued, "you want somebody who is *honest*. Life is too short for liars and smoke blowers, Bobby!"

Perfect. A one-minute phone call had sharpened my thinking one more degree, and I was grateful for it. A couple of infamous blowhards went down my priority list. I'd reach them, but if it was next week, that'd be okay!

Bradford and I agreed that we would meet with a group Friday night, and then we would meet with another group on Saturday morning. This gave me a second time slot to invite people to if they couldn't make it to the first one.

I had my marching orders.

What kind of person was I looking for?

1. Somebody who is <u>ambitious</u>
2. Somebody who is <u>looking</u> for something more in life
3. Somebody who is <u>teachable</u>
4. Somebody who is <u>honest</u>

Ambitious. Looking. Teachable. Honest.

After the call with Bradford, I sorted my list of 150 names, screening each for *ambitious*, *looking*, *teachable*, and *honest*, and by 8:00 a.m., I was ready to start my calls.

I'm a salesman. I know how to pick up the phone, dial a number, have a brief conversation, treat the person on the other end of the line like a human being, show respect and give warmth and appreciation—all the while being a human being myself—and then dial another number. Fundamental to sales is the conviction that I'm in the relationship business. The person I'm calling is a person, not a dollar sign. I believe this. I get to talk to a human being, show true appreciation, share what I'm doing, find out if he or she is interested, show more appreciation, give my respect—which every person deserves—and then do it again.

You can't lose in sales if you remember that you're not selling; you're solving problems. If you remember that and treat the person with respect, you are on the right track.

Also, you can make a ton more phone calls thinking this way!

I learned a decade and a half ago that if I'm "selling," I wear out quickly. Why? Because I can only take so many rejections in a day. If I'm selling, then every single "I'm just not interested" is a rejection. It's a "no sale!" Rack up eight or ten rejections, and my psyche is shot. How many rejections can a person take in a day? Not very many!

I did a little drinking in the afternoon hours during my first years of selling, truth be told.

And then I got it straight. I figured out how to think about my work differently. I fixed the problem that lives in the gap between my two ears, the thinking problem. I'm not selling, I realized. I'm not in the selling business. I'm in the solutions business! I'm connecting with human beings to help them solve challenges in their lives. I'm in the listening and encouraging business to learn where I can help. I call someone not to share my opportunity but rather to set a time to get together. I can't properly listen and learn to help solve problems over the phone, so the contacting step is just to set the appointment. And then, I hang up my phone and do it again. And then again.

After I got that straight, I discovered I could make a whole lot of "sales calls" in a day. Why? Because I was never rejected. Sale or no sale, every call was an opportunity for human connection to help solve problems. And if the people I called didn't currently need any problems solved, I still made a connection with them in case their situation changed in the future.

And why does this matter? Because sales really is a numbers game. That's the paradox. On one hand, it's a numbers game, but on the other, it's all about relationships. And you've got to listen to and learn from many people's stories in order to understand their specific needs and challenges because only some of them will be interested and ready—at the "Right Time" in their lives—for what you have. And if you're only thinking about the numbers, you'll stop reaching out too soon—because the rejections will be just too much to handle.

If you remember the paradox—numbers and relationships—you'll make a ton more calls. And you need to make a ton of calls to find the right people who are struggling with problems that your product can help solve at that particular moment in time.

And the by-product of getting this straight is more sales.

I became very good at what I do. And I took all of what I had learned and applied it to my new venture.

The calls went something like this.

"Hey, Barbara, this is Bobby Davis."

"Bobby, long time, no hear. How are you? How's Pam?"

"Pam's great, and I'm doing pretty well myself. Did I catch you at a bad time?"

"Not at all. What's up?"

"Great, the reason I'm calling is I fell in with a couple of leaders who have pioneered a leadership development business online. They're expanding right now, and I thought of you. I can't promise you anything, but I'm gathering a few key leaders at my house to discuss the details. Are you free either Friday night or Saturday morning?"

I either booked the appointment, or if they asked any questions like "What is it?" "Is this network marketing?" or even the dreaded "Is this one of those pyramid schemes?" they all received the same answer. Bradford had prepared me well through his coaching and the contacting audios I listened to over and over. Not everyone asked questions, but most did. Personally, I would have too. A person's time is precious, and everybody has at some point been finagled into throwing away a perfectly good evening to hear some crazy scheme.

"Have you heard of Robert Kiyosaki's **CASHFLOW Quadrant**? It'll make more sense when we get together. What day did you say was best?"

If they asked another question, I simply asked another one back, just as I learned from the contacting script and audios.

"Have you heard of Michael Dell's 3 Cs? It'll make more sense when we get together. Barbara, it's not possible for me to describe everything over the phone, but because I know Bill's and your leadership skills, I put you two at the top of my list to talk to. If you see something you like, great, and if not, no worries. The worst thing that happens is we get to catch up. What's best for you? Friday night or Saturday morning?"

More or less, that was how my phone calls went.

And even if a "No" was a true "No," I still always treated the people with dignity. They were human beings, after all, intrinsically respectable. Who was I to know what other people should want to do with their precious time? I promised myself to meet every "No" with posture and courtesy for the fact that they had answered the phone to begin with.

By noon on Friday, I had twelve friends coming over for an 8:00 p.m. gathering in my home that night and another eight coming on Saturday morning. I had hoped for twice as many, but my ambitions are always bigger than my results. Hope springs eternal!

The other thing I did all week was follow the reading and listening plan that Bradford had given me. Reading every day reignited my mind and heart toward the goals I had set. Listening to the CDs and Rascal Radio audios on my iPhone gave me concrete example after concrete example from men and women who were out there doing it. These disciplines were cleaning out my mind's damaged messages of defeat and helplessness and keeping me encouraged and refreshed. I couldn't wait to catch up with Bradford and learn how to turn this into a powerful routine that I could track and manage; he told me that he would show me how to do this and how to teach it to others.

I picked Bradford up from the Dallas/Fort Worth International Airport at 4:30 on Friday afternoon. He had a noon flight back to Detroit the next day, and I was going to make the most of his generosity.

"How's it looking, Bobby?" he asked.

"I've got twelve tonight for you, Bradford," I began. "I had wanted twenty-five, but it's a good group that are coming over."

He gave me a measured gaze.

"And eight tomorrow morning," I added, feeling very inadequate.

"Well done, Bobby!" Bradford gushed. "I know how hard you worked to pull that off!" His words were spoken with conviction. And I *had* worked hard. Not for a second had I forgotten Pam. I'd called again and again, a picture of my beloved wife propped up against the lamp on my desk to goad me into keeping at my task. I wasn't just trying to build a business, after all. I was trying to rebuild a life. And Pam was at the heart of my life.

We had some informal time as the men and women—mostly in couples—arrived at my home Friday evening. I offered them some snacks and drinks and chitchatted a bit with them but also respected their time. Shortly after 8:00 p.m., I assembled everyone into the living room and rounded up some extra chairs to accommodate everybody. I had already placed a portable whiteboard that Bradford had asked for by the TV set since I knew he would be our educational entertainment for the night.

"Ladies and gentlemen," I began, "when I called you and asked you to join me tonight, I promised to share some details on one of the fastest growing leadership companies in the world. To do this, I am pulling out the big guns. Tonight, I have the distinct honor of introducing you to my good friend and mentor, Bradford Henderson!"

Some of my guests clapped, while others seemed to be soaking it all in.

"How many of you have heard of Robert Kiyosaki's *CASHFLOW Quadrant*?" Bradford began. A few hands went up. "And what do you remember about it?" he asked one of the men who had raised his hand.

"A few people make all the money," the man answered. "The guy was a genius!" he added. Several of my guests chuckled.

Bradford outright laughed. If there was fun to be had, he wanted a piece of it. "That's what we remember the easiest about Kiyosaki," he affirmed, smiling broadly. "Five percent of the people earn ninety-five percent of the money. Kind of sticks in your mind, doesn't it!"

Bradford was grinning as he looked from face to face, and his warmth and good humor were infectious. He was a regular guy, and nothing was put on about him. And I saw that my guests were already settling in. Faces were open, people were grinning right back at Bradford, and heads were nodding along.

"But Kiyosaki was saying something a lot more objectionable about the way we live our lives than that 95 percent of us get stuck with only 5 percent of the money. Don't get me wrong. I think that part stinks plenty bad all by itself!" More chuckles. Bradford's eyes were dancing with mirth. He was deadly serious about his topic but still enjoying himself immensely.

He turned to the white board and wrote four big letters in a square, like this:

"This is Kiyosaki's *CASHFLOW Quadrant*. The 'E' stands for 'Employee' — which means that you have a job.

---

* Robert Kiyosaki created this "ESBI" model in his **New York Times** best-selling business and entrepreneurship book **Rich Dad's CASHFLOW Quadrant** (Plata Publishing, 2011).

You trade your time for a paycheck." Bradford scanned the room for a second to make sure he wasn't going too fast.

"The 'S' stands for 'Self-Employed'—which means that you *own* a job. You might have some employees working for you, but the day you take off is the day your sales drop or your customers don't get as good service as when you're there. You're still trading your time for a paycheck." Another scan of the room. Some of the men had lost their grins.

"And the 95 percent who make 5 percent of the money are the Es and the Ss. It's always an exchange of your time for money, and folks," Bradford's face had turned sober for the very first time, "time matters more than money. On the left-hand side of the quadrant, you never get a break." Now there wasn't a grin in the room.

"What I find more objectionable than 95 percent of the money going to 5 percent of the people is how many good and decent men and women there are who, in fact, make a very good living but who have to spend ninety hours a week doing it. And all the while, their kids are growing up so fast that their childhoods are passing by like a blink.

"Selling your time for money is not something I like—at *any* price, even if you're one of the so-called lucky ones who gets a lot of money for your time.

"You might own your own business in the legal sense, what I call a 'Self-Business,' but if it's just a bigger treadmill that you can't get off, you still haven't solved life's biggest issue, which is a time issue. Make sense?" he asked.

Nods all around.

"And over here on the right is a 'B,' which stands for 'Business,' what I call a 'B-Type Business'—a true business—'cause it actually runs while you and your family are back-packing in the Rocky Mountains. A business is a true 'B' business when you do two things: 1) develop people and 2) own a system that people can use to produce results even when you're not there. And it's this 'B' business quadrant that I want to talk to you about tonight. J. Paul Getty described a 'B' business best when he said the key to wealth is to learn how to make money while you sleep. The only way to do this is through people and systems development. Do you see the difference between an 'S' business and a 'B' business?"

I could practically see the crowd picking up the concepts. "What's the 'I' stand for?"

"Oh," Bradford said, laughing, "the 'I' stands for the people who make their money through 'Investments.' I usually skip that one because few people have an extra five hundred thousand dollars lying around to qualify to play in this quadrant. Plus, for me, it's just more fun to lead people to succeed in the 'B' quadrant than it is to manage portfolios in the 'I' quadrant. And so I pay professionals to invest for me, and the rest I hand over to my wife. She takes it from there!"

"Smart man!" one of the women chortled. Several female elbows found their way into neighboring male ribcages. Bradford's grin was back on full display.

"So to summarize, the 'E' and the 'S' on the left-hand side depend entirely on your time. You have a job, or you own a job. Either way, as Kiyosaki points out, it's a J.O.B." Bradford wrote these letters down the left side of the board. "And Kiyosaki says that 'J.O.B.' stands for 'Just Over Broke.' Current data shows that 75 percent of the population have less than $5,000 in the bank for retirement, and after retirement, only 2 percent have what they need to be self-sustaining. Everybody else is depending on relatives, hoping for social security, leaning on charity, or still working. Anybody else concerned about that?" he added.

Vigorous nods all around the room, this time without smiles.

"And on the right side, here," he said, "everything is based on leadership of people and a system that amplifies your labors, your talents, and your efforts, leveraging what you bring to the table into something more. And," Bradford continued, almost shouting, "the system always has continuation built in. Amplification! Continuation! That's how the 5 percent think, and that's how the 5 percent win. Just as John D. Rockefeller is credited with saying, 'I would rather earn 1% off a 100 people's efforts than 100% of my own efforts.'[1] Only people who make money on the right side of the quadrant have the time left to live their dreams. What, in other words, is the point of working so hard, if you never get to enjoy some of the fruits of your labors? This is why having a purpose and having a plan are so essential to success."

Bradford Henderson had already made good on my promise to my friends and associates. Nobody would walk out at the end of the evening feeling that they had wasted their time. I could almost see the wheels turning in their minds. The information they had already received would change some of their lives.

"But I didn't come here to show you Robert Kiyosaki's *CASHFLOW Quadrant*, folks," Bradford continued, erasing his chicken scratchings from the white board. "I came here to show you a business that allows people to live their purpose. And I know, when I am finished, you'll understand why it has changed so many people's personal and financial situations. That's why I do this, ladies and gentlemen. I want to change lives! In fact, our rules for business are to have fun, make money, and make a difference. Who wouldn't enjoy business under those rules?"

More nods.

"The short version, folks, is that we merchandise information to help people live the life they've always wanted to live. Period, end of story. We merchandise this information in all kinds of formats: books, CDs, DVDs, smartphone apps, live seminars, you name it. What's important isn't the *how* but the *what*. Our product is life-changing information, delivered monthly to your house. Daily wisdom nuggets compound over time into huge changes in a person's life. We address the top areas people identify that are important to them, touching family, their money, their health and fitness, their leadership, how to build friendships, and so forth.

"Most people I know could stand to grow in one or more of these categories. True?" Bradford asked. Heads nodded.

"And here's what's interesting. We know historically that right thinking leads to right actions, which in turn lead to changed lives. And how do human beings take in the kind of right thinking they need to get better results?" he asked. "Little by little," he then answered, holding up his pointer finger. "Right thinking..." he continued, shaking his pointer to underscore this first point and raising his middle finger to join it, "correctly applied..." scanning the room to be sure everybody was tracking and then raising his ring finger to join the lineup, "in small doses..." adding the pinky finger, "over time. That, folks, is how we grow: right information, correctly applied, in small doses, over time!

"So many people think they can spend five thousand dollars and fly to Vegas for the weekend and become a leader. This simply isn't the way a person develops leadership. In reality, the only way to develop leadership is through serving people, not mastering a ropes course or walking on hot coals."

Heads were shaking and laughter rippled through the room. It looked to me as if some of these guys had bought that Vegas leadership program themselves a time or two. And they knew that Bradford was telling it like it is.

"True information, folks, correctly applied, in small doses, over time. Great leaders from throughout history made themselves lifelong learners, readers, and students of life. Cyrus the Great, who liberated the Jews to return to Jerusalem, Caesar Augustus, who united the Roman Empire out of its thousand splinters, George Washington, who led thirteen colonies through the perils of birthing a nation, Winston Churchill, who stood tall in the blitzkrieg of World War II—these were men of continual, intentional reading and learning.

"And we conquer our own troubles and seize our own opportunities in the very same way: through continual, bite-sized, intentional learning. Our company serves its customers by delivering the life-changing information they need, in ways that people can absorb, on a steady, monthly drumbeat, so that men, women, youth, and children can learn how to live the life that they've always wanted to live. Like the Good Book says, 'as [a man] thinks, so is he.'[2] Change the way you think, and you change your life. The crazy part about LIFE Leadership is we actually get paid to change our own lives and then others' lives. It's called 'compensated communities,' and it's a lot of fun!"

When the presentation ended, no one rushed for the door. Instead, the comments and questions jumped around like grasshoppers. But because Bradford was a professional, he had already answered most of the common questions and objections (How is the money made? How do you learn how to do the business? How much does it cost to join? Are people making money? Is this a pyramid?) during the plan. For the most part, people were talking about their dreams and how to get started. Bradford was clear and straightforward with his answers and thoughts. There was no smoke and mirrors. He provided a few handouts, links to an information-packed website, and lots of humor and encouragement.

"At the end of the day," Bradford concluded, "joining Bobby and me is fundamentally about joining a leadership community that teaches how to build effective leaders and systems. You'll lean on Bobby, for sure, but the whole company is at your fingertips through our training system—at *your* fingertips *and* at the fingertips of each person you reach out to.

"Success is the progressive realization of a worthwhile goal or dream. You'll learn a ton on this journey and become a better person in the process. That is what true success is about," he added, looking around the room, making eye contact, and deeply connecting with my guests. "I don't promise you easy."

Heads were nodding. It didn't look to me like anybody was in the market for easy.

"But I do promise you 'worth it!' You can hold me to that, folks. This is a company that makes a true difference. And the work will be worth it!

"So for those who are interested, here are the next steps."

Bradford had everybody's attention. It looked to me as though a number of people were getting their guards up to beat back the sales pitch, the hard close. I watched and felt very proud already of this company and of the way it operated.

"Number one, take the first-night information that Bobby has for you: some CDs and an easy-reading book.

There is no way anyone can learn this business in just over an hour! Take the time to listen to the CDs and read the book. It will make a ton more sense to those who do.

"Two, come back tomorrow morning or set a time to get back together with Bobby to talk things over. There is never a convenient time to make changes in a person's life. Winners simply make the time. Get back together with Bobby in the next few days. Keep tonight fresh.

"Three, our company holds weekly Open Meetings here in Dallas and in cities across North America. There's one here next Tuesday night. Get to it. Put yourself into learner's mode. Right information, correctly applied, in small doses, over time. Make room to learn and master this!

"And four, if any of you are ready to hold your spot, you can sign up tonight for under one hundred dollars. Who starts a business with so much potential for less? Bobby and I will back up our talk with our walk. Let's get started, shall we?"

ACTION STEP 3: SERVE COOKIES AND CREAM

It's late Sunday evening, and I've had little time since Bradford was with me Friday evening and Saturday morning to update these notes. Let me start with what matters most.

Late last evening, Pam called.

It should have occurred to me that Chrissie Henderson was going to stay in touch with Pam. And it should have dawned on me that Pam would learn about the results of Bradford's visit with me here in Dallas. I don't mean that there was a spy operation going on; there wasn't, strictly speaking. But I already believed to the bottom of my heart that Pam was on my side, that she was taking a hard line with me because she knew that change was necessary, for me, for her, and for us. I already believed that she was keeping her distance precisely for the purpose of protecting the pain and the pregnancy of this moment, this transformational moment.

If Pam had rushed in a week ago, I fear that I would have fallen into familiar pathways: self-recrimination, lament, self-pity, a search for solace, and ultimately, flat-footedness. I must say, in all truth, that I don't think Pam ever considered rushing in and easing my pain a week ago. I think she contemplated only two courses of action: 1) leave me for good (because she couldn't and wouldn't play this defeatist game for the rest of her life) or 2) leave me alone (because she knew that this was her and my and our family's only true hope).

She chose to leave me alone because, well, she made a wedding vow to never forsake me, not until death itself. It's a little ironic because really she sort of did forsake me, in faithfulness to her vows before God never to forsake me. I have believed this all week long, and I took up my work this week as her partner, her mate, doing what I could to learn my part in this urgent and essential marriage dance that we were staggering our way through—a dance for our renewal.

Since I already believed this, it should have occurred to me that she would keep tabs on me—that she'd be a watchwoman for any sign that I was, finally, on her team and that I was stepping up and stepping in, joining her in our new and very awkward dance. She was trying to learn some new steps. Of course she'd be desperate to discover if I was trying too.

And so, Bradford flew home. And, of course, Chrissie asked him to share about his time with me, which he did. And then she went straightaway to the phone and called Pam and told her what was going on.

Women can be so incredibly wise and circumspect and artful. And they can suffer with such grace and, as needs be, silence.

"Pam!" I had answered, hoping it was her on her line and not her dad again.

"Bobby," she responded, her voice quavering. "I miss you, Bobby," she then managed to add.

And I was undone. She missed me. I had believed it all week. I couldn't afford to believe anything else, even as I had been fearing the very opposite of what I believed. But she was telling me now. She missed me.

"And I miss you, Pam!" I blurted out. "I love you so much!"

I'm not going to write out all that we next said to each other, partly because most of it is sacred and partly because some of it was really clumsy. And, frankly, it's mostly nobody's business but Pam's and mine.

We talked for a long time.

She told me that Chrissie's report provided her with her first ray of hope in a very long time. "Bradford really bragged on you, Bobby," she said. "You've been working your butt off and really going for it!"

And that's what she's been wanting from me—not that I do this or that but that I step up, grow up, man up. She knew that our family was never going to be okay if no one was willing to be the man. And it killed her to watch me twist round and round my flagpole of excuses and regrets.

She knew, more than any other human being on earth, that my deepest heart's dream was to build a business of my own, to venture out from the confines and the cover of an employer and to stake a claim, draw a line in the sand, and stand on the front of that line.

And she had watched me shrink back from this dream time and again, shrink back and fail to follow through on the disciplines and the behaviors that success demanded. In short, Pam had watched my fears consume my dreams, and what this always looked like in the past was me not taking action, me hesitating, me holding back.

On our call, Pam also updated me on our kids, who were in seventh heaven, even if they were missing their dad. She shared several hilarious stories of their antics, including that my oldest son, Rob, happened to bump into the fifteen-year-old daughter of the farmer next door (whose family happens to attend the same church as my parents-in-law) and had just checked with his mother for the fourth time if they were, for sure, planning to go to church the next morning.

My blood raced when I heard this story. My children are growing so fast. I'd been trading all my time for money their whole life. It had to stop!

"Always a very religious boy," was what I actually said, my voice in deadpan.

"Very religious!" Pam agreed, her voice regaining colors that I hadn't heard there in quite a while.

And I updated Pam on what had transpired, giving her my angle on the time with Bradford and on my back-to-back meetings through the remainder of Saturday. In fact, I had just finished my last visit, stopping over at Barbara and Bill Baxter's house to sign them up and "get them on the train."

In all, Bradford presented our company to twenty individuals in his twenty hours in Dallas. And he walked me through the sign-up process with two of the couples who were ready to get started immediately. "We've been looking for something like this and already checked out a number of alternatives. This is the one," they said, "so let's go!"

"Looking," Bradford reminded me. "Ambitious, looking, teachable, and honest. They were already looking!"

I paid three more visits to people who had come to my house — after I put Bradford back on his plane — signed up Barbara and Bill, and had just gotten home when Pam's call came.

Pam also revealed to me what she was thinking. It wasn't an edict this time; it was her thinking. And she was looking for my thoughts on the matter.

"What kind of a week is ahead of you, Bobby?" she began, her voice tentative.

"Pam, I can drop everything," I stammered, misunderstanding the direction of her inquiry. "You and the kids come first! What do you want me to do?"

"Bobby," she began again, "I'm not asking you to do anything. I'm asking you what kind of a week you're looking at."

I backed up a step and decided to answer her question.

"Packed," I answered. And I winced. With my family so strained, was this the time for me to pack a week full of work?

"I can reschedule," I blurted again.

"Packed with what?" she replied, as though I had not just spoken.

"Showing the plan, Pam," I answered. "Two more follow-throughs Monday, an evening meeting with several friends of one of the couples that we signed up on Friday night, and more phone calls; I'm trying to fill another Friday evening and Saturday morning. My list is bigger than when I started my calls on Wednesday, and now I'm helping three new couples build their businesses.

"Plus," I continued, thinking that I may as well get it all out, "it's end of quarter at work, Pam, and though my numbers are great, I've got a few important contacts to make and some paperwork to do for my boss.

"I planned to work every evening this week," I added apologetically.

"I didn't foresee you calling me just yet, Pam!" My feelings of contrition were bottomless. "I wouldn't have done it this way!"

I held my breath.

"So, Bobby," Pam began, her voice radiating equanimity. "Your week and my thoughts seem to be in complete alignment."

I pressed my phone harder into my eardrum. I needed to be sure I was getting this right.

"I was thinking that the kids and I could fly home next Sunday — after church, of course! I don't want to deny our son's life of prayer!

"My thought, Bobby, was that you could use another week of new habit building," she added, a tentativeness in her voice. "I mean no disrespect, darling," she added, "but I want to see more of you pressing in hard like this."

I breathed. And then I smiled. I knew she couldn't see it, but I was grinning ear to ear. And there was a tear in my eye. I had been right. Pam was on my team, and she was playing her part brilliantly — and very courageously, too.

And it was agreed. I'd keep working my butt off. And my family would be home in a week. Well, most of my family. I had a feeling that I'd get back one very moon-faced fifteen-year-old boy whose heart, maybe, wouldn't be making the trip.

*   *   *   *

I had planned to keep my notes in this journal up to date every day, but as you can see, I've been falling off. Sunday evening was the last I wrote — catching up on my weekend with Bradford, the follow-through's I got done after the

Friday night and Saturday morning presentations, and my call with Pam.

And now it's Wednesday night. I'm shaking my head! I have been on a learning curve and at the very same time inside a tornado since I last sat down to write.

When Bradford left my car Saturday at noon, he asked me to do the follow-throughs we had agreed to, to keep the press on both myself and the couples who had joined my team to make new appointments, and to get to the Tuesday evening Open Meeting that he asked my guests to please attend. His final words to me were, "Get me on a video call first thing Monday, Bobby! I don't care which technology platform we use for the call. Just make it happen! It's absolutely time for your next lesson. We'll do <u>Action Step Number 3</u>. And trust me that you need to learn this one immediately!"

And on that (both emphatic and enigmatic) note, Bradford had turned and hustled himself into the airport.

We jumped onto Google Hangout late in the morning on Monday. He was smiling when the screen came alive.

"Chrissie gave me an update on you and Pam," he began. "I really like what I hear!"

I just smiled. I liked what I was hearing, too. What I was watching. It all felt so orchestrated. Providential. Merciful, even.

I bumped into Bradford Henderson at a grocery store, which precipitated the biggest crisis of my marriage—or brought the building crisis that was my marriage to a head, to its crescendo—and then Bradford's wife stepped in, perfectly prepositioned to counsel and encourage Pam while Bradford coached and encouraged me. So much of this was beyond my control that all I could do was show my thankfulness through my efforts.

And because of my efforts, I felt more hopeful than I had in years.

I was busting a gut to stand on the battle lines of my life — not tucked behind the ramparts this time but out in front with my troops, directly in the line of fire and leading the charge. Meanwhile, Pam was guarded and secure, guided by the wisest of counsel. She would hold the home and the family, maintain the wall of unbreachable defense — for me and for the Davis family — that would allow me to pour every ounce of my energy into claiming an entirely new piece of ground for us to own and occupy. I could pour myself into this venture precisely because I knew that she had my back.

Bradford saw my smile, and his smile doubled.

"It's about love and care, Bobby!"

"It is about love and care, Bradford," I answered. "Pam and I are learning some very new things about this just now, about what love and care demand of each of us."

Bradford gave it a beat and just kept smiling.

"Beautiful," he said, nodding his head once.

"And our lesson this morning is about love and care," he added, transitioning as smoothly as a sunrise.

I threw my transmission into drive, heard the whir and felt the sync of the gears, and prepared myself to absorb the torque of Bradford's teaching.

"Action Step 3: Serve Cookies and Cream," Bradford launched, "is all about love and care. Many are called, Bobby, but few are chosen." I wondered where I had heard that line before. "We just got your head straight about the fact that people will join this company telling you they're ready to work hard but that they may or may not actually be ready. Right?"

I nodded vigorously.

"And it's all good! Worst-case scenario is that people join and do absolutely nothing, but at least they're starting to read good books and listen to good talks. Not bad, right?"

I agreed with a nod of my head. Not bad at all. Good, rather. Very good!

Yet I still wasn't feeling the direction of Bradford's instruction.

"So some of your newer people will do what you do, follow where you lead, learn the system, and master the simple, repeatable behaviors that will lead them to success. And some of them won't."

Okay. That was established.

"And as you get them started, you won't know which new colleagues are going to be which."

Correct. That would be correct. I already didn't know who, of my first three couples who had signed up, would actually do anything.

"But whether they do or don't do what success requires, Bobby, you are going to love them like crazy, care for them, and serve them! You hear me?"

A command was never more commandingly given. I heard him.

"They claimed their seat on your train. And in a minute, you're going to find out how to begin the process of teaching them how to own and drive and build their own train. But right now, day one, you begin to serve your people."

"Cookies and cream?" I asked.

"A figure of speech. A word picture. You took your own seat on the train. You are now helping others get on the train. In a minute, I'm going to show you how to move the train on down the tracks—how to build momentum and excitement—but you don't have to wait a single second to begin to serve those you've brought on board. Serve them cookies and cream!"

"How do I do that?" I asked. I loved the practicality of this. Something I could do immediately was very appealing to me. The idea of inviting people to hold their spot on the train but then having to wait for a while for something else to happen left me feeling very uneasy.

"If I may, Bobby," Bradford began, "I'll be both very specific and very general—specific so you have marching orders you know how to follow and general so you know the principle of the thing and can make up new kinds of specific examples as you proceed. Make sense?"

It made perfect sense!

"Make sure your new colleagues get to the Tuesday Open Meeting tomorrow night. Tell them ahead of time that you want to take them out for coffee or ice cream afterward. Got that?"

I nodded.

"All kinds of business happens in business, Bobby. You and your partners are hard at work, rotating the pattern of making a list, contacting, showing the plan, following through, and helping them get started as a customer or member. I know you're working to help bring some of their new people to the Open. You're doing the work and helping others do the same. But the work is only part of the work.

"In fact, I would say all of business is relationships because ultimately it's the people who are the decision makers in every company. As a result, whenever a company mistreats its people in order to complete its tasks, the organization begins its decline. The best business leaders, in other words, build people who then complete the tasks to help build the business. Make it a habit to take your team out to coffee after Open Meetings and Monthly Seminars. Do this from the start, and never stop doing it. This is vital because you've got to make it clear that, first and foremost, your business relationship is a *human* relationship. We are friends who happen to be in business. Yes, there's work to do, but never forget you're friends first and business partners second.

"Serve them cookies and cream!"

I more than got it. The consistency of this with everything else I believed about business was huge. My sales calls were relationship touches. Why should that stop once we had the privilege of getting to work together?

"Everybody on earth is starved for a real, loving human relationship, Bobby. So few people have a true friend who would get out of bed at 3:00 a.m. to help them if they were stranded somewhere. It's sad but true. We can change that. Remember, we're a 'life-changing information company.' How about we actually practice the principles we are learning from the audios and books? What if we truly display love and care for one another while we go about building our 'life-changing information company'? Perhaps that's what Gandhi meant when he said be the change you wish to see in the world."

Yes, indeed.

"From the very first touch, you're a servant, Bobby. We covered that. And now that you have people on your train, you've got to engage them in the system that makes this all work. Association with like-minded people changes people from the inside out. Everyone knows this intuitively. For example, there is an old Southern saying that says if you hang out with dogs, you get fleas. In a compensated community, it's the opposite: if you hang out with dreamers, you get dreams. As people attend Tuesday night Opens and Saturday seminars, they become part of a leadership culture that teaches them how to face their Goliaths in life and beat them. This is crucial because it provides the training, reinforcement, encouragement, counsel, and discipline that are needed. It's our system, and you want your people to be fully engaged in all of it so that they aren't depending on just you for everything!"

"Because if they were just leaning on me, I'd have an S-Type Business—a Self-Business. I'd stay part of the 95 percent who live on 5 percent of the wealth. I wouldn't have a real business, a B-Type Business that I can actually depend on to run whether I'm there or not." I was showing Bradford that I got Kiyosaki's *CASHFLOW* lesson.

"Yes!" he practically shouted. "Never invest in a business where the system goes home at night; that is an 'S' business. An 'S' business is limited to how much time the business owner can afford to invest in it. But a true 'B' business is different. It is scalable to millions of people because it doesn't rely on the business owner's time as much as it does his leadership and the power of a scalable system that can teach millions. Just remember this, Bobby. While you're plugging people into the training system and teaching them to rely on it for answers, remember that what makes the people side work is love and encouragement from the leader. That leader is *you*, Bobby! Love and encouragement are the oil that lubricates the training system to effectively produce leaders."

"Cookies and cream," I added.

"Cookies and cream!" Bradford nearly barked. "By the way, this isn't just some technique. A leader's character, love, and respect must come from his heart, not just his head. What do you respect and admire in your teammates? Invest time with your leaders after every event. Ask them to share about their dreams. Praise them. Remind them of why they got started in the first place. Ask them to tell each other what they're longing to achieve. Have fun with them. Teach them how to serve each other through your example…and encourage them to do the same. Without reciprocating character, love, and respect amongst the leaders, the system quickly falters upon the rock of broken trust. Leadership is character and love in motion!

"How do you spell love, Bobby?" he then asked.

"L-O-V-E," I answered.

Bradford laughed hard, a real and joyful laugh. He was having true fun working alongside me. And I was getting his point. He wanted me to have true fun working alongside my people.

"T-I-M-E, Bobby. You spell it T-I-M-E!"

"And E-N-C-O-U-R-A-G-E-M-E-N-T," I added.

"Yes, T-I-M-E and E-N-C-O-U-R-A-G-E-M-E-N-T…and F-U-N and S-H-A-R-I-N-G and D-E-S-S-E-R-T." We both laughed. A couple of spelling champions, we were! "You take your friends out after the meeting to grab a coffee. You show love and care to your people by taking your colleagues out for time together *after* the work session — because they mean more to you than the work! It's them that you're dedicated to. Build your people, and your people will build your business! Clear?"

It was clear.

And troubling.

Did my kids know that my work was in service to them? How well did Pam know that my work was in service to her? It was! My work was in service to my wife and kids.

But did they know that? Or did they think that my work was what I loved, what I served, what I cared about and that they, my wife and kids, were part of the supporting cast, secondary players, disposable extras?

Bradford and I finished the call. But instead of jumping into my to-do list, I sat in a trance. A "life-changing information company"! I think I just got a fire-hose dose of it myself.

My new members weren't the only ones who were about to get some life-changing information! My wife and kids were about to get some too.

And how would I deliver this new, life-changing information? Cookies and cream would make a great start!

CHAPTER 8

ACTION STEP 4: MOVE THE TRAIN

"Bradford!" I practically shouted.

It amuses me how primitive we actually are. We have extraordinary technology and can get "face to face" with human beings who are twelve time zones away, and yet we don't actually need to shout to be heard. It isn't like we have to communicate across the Grand Canyon, booming out our message in slow, measured syllables to control the confusing echo that will be created by the vast canyon walls that surround us. We could actually just whisper if we wanted, and it would work as well as if we were sitting elbow to elbow on the couch.

Our primitiveness kicks right in, nonetheless, especially when we're excited, confused, or amazed. We forget that our smartphone can be trusted to carry our ordinary speaking voice from Dallas to Detroit, with no shouting required.

"You signed the Ruscittos up late Friday night after our meeting, and then you signed the Painters up as customers! They still might join the company but really wanted to start using the books and audios to help them improve their life. And on Saturday, I signed Bill and Barbara Baxter into the Ruscittos' business!" I was still shouting.

"Correct," Bradford said, confirming that I was reading my website correctly. Plain as day, I could see each of these new business associates listed within my team, each one of them now part of the muscle of the enterprise that I was building. And they were already providing muscle to one another. In fact, the Ruscittos and Baxters stood a very good chance of adding several new customers and members to their businesses that very day, so I was looking forward to even more growth, and they'd enjoy the growth just like me!

"But who are the Eddings and the Sabags and the Otts?" I then asked, still shouting but now revealing the source of all this volume.

"I haven't looked at your activity, Bobby," Bradford answered. His voice was regular volume. He, apparently, believed that the telephone company knew how to do its job. "But the Sabags are a couple I signed up last night. They live in Naples, Florida. And I'm guessing that the Eddings and the Otts came from a house meeting that Don and Doris had at their house last evening. You'll meet Don and Doris tonight, since they're part of your support team and live just down the road from you in Austin. They're a terrific leadership couple, and I asked them to show the plan for you tonight—which will let you see another example of how to share the plan to help get you ready to show it yourself next time." Bradford's voice remained calm. He spoke as someone who was patiently explaining to a Romulan that, indeed, the sun does come up each and every day, for this is how things work here on planet Earth.

"My company is twice the size of what I actually built!" I stammered. "I know you said it works this way, but I didn't *know* that it worked this way!"

I could almost hear the smile in Bradford's voice. "And how does this make you feel, Bobby?" he asked.

"It makes me feel…like…wow!" I answered. So emotionally intelligent, I am. "Wow" is not technically a feeling. What can I say? I'm a guy!

"So, Bobby," Bradford continued, "I urged you to 'Get On the Train' and hold your spot. Remember?"

I remembered.

"And why did I tell you to hold your spot?" "Professor Socrates" was in full flower.

"So that I'd have one?" I ventured.

Bradford laughed. "You think I asked you to 'Get On the Train' and hold your spot so you could have a spot on the train?" He was the one now who apparently didn't trust the phone company to carry his voice across the thousand miles that separated us.

"Well, yeah," I answered lamely. Why was he shouting? Didn't he know this was the twenty-first century?

"I told you to hold your spot because I knew the train was exiting the station! I and everybody else in your support team are hard at work. You get to ride along and learn the process while you experience the progress—but only if you're actually sitting on the train when it moves.

"Let me ask you again," he continued. "You've been working your butt off, all last week setting up our Friday and Saturday meetings and all this week going to the Open on Tuesday, following up with your people, and getting them geared up with their own people for the meeting you're going to have tonight. You told me that you've got another ten people coming to your house tonight, right? Ten, not counting the Baxters and the Ruscittos?"

That's what I told him. Tonight, Friday night, one week after Bradford had flown in to lead my meeting, I had sixteen people lined up, my six teammates plus ten potential members/customers, which Bradford referred to as "prospects." But this time, there were people coming who had been invited by *my* people, not just by me.

"So tonight, Don and Doris will present the plan like I presented it last week. Only tonight, you've got six couples already on your team and building the business even though you only personally invited three of the couples. Plus, your people each have people inside their team—the Eddings and the Sabags and the Otts—who are part of their team thanks to us building with a Team Approach. I LOVE win–win. And so now, you get to tell your people that I've been working for them this week and that Don and Doris, whom they don't even know yet, have also been working for them.

"Do you see how this is different? You're in business *for* yourself, Bobby, but not *by* yourself!

"So how does this make you feel?"

The first time he asked that, I said, "like...wow," which I now realize was totally inadequate.

"Bradford, it makes me feel like I could bust straight through a concrete barricade! It makes me feel like I was told something that was just too good to be true, and then I found out that it absolutely was true!"

"I'm asking you this question, Bobby, to help you get your heart around what's going on," Bradford continued. "Is it a stretch to say that you feel more confident now?"

"No stretch!" I exclaimed. "Are you kidding me?"

"And what does feeling more confident do for you, Bobby?" Mr. Bradford "Socrates" Henderson continued.

"It makes me want to get out there and work harder!" I replied. "It makes me realize that I can do this! It shifts everything around from 'I think this might work' to 'This works!' It makes me hungry to do more—*much* more!"

"Perfect!" Bradford declared. His voice conveyed his deep joy in my answers to his questions. "We are a team—together, everyone achieves more—orchestrating a Team Approach.

"Ready for your next lesson?"

I was ready.

"Step 1 was Get On the Train," he began. I pulled out my notebook and flipped to the page where I had been writing down each of the steps.

"Step 2 was Get Others onto the Train. And Step 3 was Serve Cookies and Cream. I told you to grab yourself a seat, and I showed you how to help other people get themselves a seat right there with you. And then I emphasized the importance of showing love and care to everybody who joins you, right from the get-go. Correct?"

This was exactly what I had written down. And it was what I was doing and teaching. Tonight, Bill and Barbara Baxter, the Ruscittos, and the Painters would be at my house because I had worked Step 1, Step 2, and Step 3. Tuesday night after the Open, I took them out for coffee, and we had a blast. I asked them simple questions, encouraged them to tell their stories to each other, and watched in amazement as they bonded. People are so hungry for connection, for true community. I'm so hungry for it, too!

And the result was that my team invited six of the ten new people coming tonight! My team was doing what I had taught them, following the disciplines and the behaviors—following the system—and it was bearing fruit.

Plus, tonight, I would get to tell them that they already had new people on their teams who were building depth for them, who were out there marketing the great informational products we bring to the world (to the benefit of *my* people) and who would bring even more people into the organization by placing them in the group (to the benefit of everybody who had, so far, grabbed themselves a seat).

I already knew that this was going to light a fire in more people than me.

"So why did I work so hard to get your train moving, Bobby?" Bradford then asked. "Why did I and Don and Doris go to great lengths to move your train and not just rest on the fact that you had moved *our* trains, which we loved? Why did we in your support team keep working so that your train would move?"

"Well," I began.

"And why," Bradford interrupted, "are you going to work like crazy to keep bringing new people into *your* team, placing them underneath the people who already grabbed their seat? And why are you going to teach each of your people to do this? And then, when you bring yet newer people in, why are you going to work hard to move *their* trains, to get still more people to join within *their* organizations?"

"Because it builds the company?" I ventured.

"Yes, it builds the company," Bradford responded. "But there's an even better answer, and you, of all people, should know what it is!"

I took a breath and reflected on what I, indeed, did already know. And I shook my head in amazement.

"You worked so hard to move the train because it builds *me*," I then answered more slowly. "You and Don and Doris worked so hard because you're building me."

"And let me repeat myself, Bobby. Why will you work so hard to get each of your people's trains moving—to be able to show them that they are making real progress, and to do this within a few days of their joining, while they're still wondering whether they can do it or if it actually works?"

"I'll do this because it builds them," I answered.

"Builds their what?" Bradford asked.

"Confidence. Trust. Excitement. Energy. Passion," I replied.

"I can sum it up in one world, Bobby: BELIEF! And belief creates momentum, which leads to growth, while lack of belief creates lack of momentum, which leads to decline. Napoleon said it best: 'A leader is a dealer in hope,'[1] and building depth (moving the train) builds belief and hope for the future. I told you that we serve our people cookies and cream because we're their leaders. We serve them. We love them. We're in it for them, and we pour in the love and encouragement. This is what true leadership is about: modeling and messaging."

I was writing as fast as I could, and my head was nodding like a bobblehead going across a railroad yard.

"And now I'm telling you that we <u>Move the Train</u>—we do our utmost to always make progress and show progress in our company—for the very same reason. We do it because we're our peoples' servants. We serve them. We love them. We're in it for them. Only now, our love and service is of a different kind than the cookies-and-cream kind."

"Now we're lighting their fire!" I nearly shouted. "We're turning on their humanity! We are getting them out of their helpless state, out of their coma of complacency, out of their thumb-sucking, excuse-making state, and moving them into action, into belief, into full drive!"

I did know what I was talking about! My fire was lit. Well, Pam lit it, in my case, but now Bradford poured a drum of gasoline onto the fire. This was a very different kind of service than the "what will you do for me?" kind. This was the kind of service that awakened the heart of a dragon slayer, shook off the chains of the oppressed, and gave new sight to the blind and fleet-footedness to the crippled.

Bradford had intentionally moved my train this week, not because it served *him*, though it did, but because it served *me*. I got it!

I had just joined a "life-changing leadership company." For sure, I had. And suddenly I realized that I *was* the company's product. They were bringing into the world a way better me! And they were also compensating me in the process. It occurred to me that this is why Bradford had said this was much more than a network marketing company. It truly was a *compensated community*, and everything they were building into me, I would build into others. I could help bring out the best versions of the people I served. Courageous versions. Heroic versions.

I could invite others to build their own compensated community, and then I could serve them, grow them, and watch them become the people that they were meant to be.

"Who would ever want to sleep, Bradford?" I asked. My mind was racing. "How would you ever know that you've done enough? Honestly, I could do this work day and night!"

"Perfect!" Bradford crowed. "Our lesson today is called <u>Action Step 4: Move the Train.</u> We've built this into the system, Bobby. Grab your seat: One. Bring others onto the train with you: Two. Serve them cookies and cream: Three. And then get that train moving: Four! You want your people to be settling into their seats and starting to familiarize themselves with how everything works, and then before they even expect it, the scenery outside their window changes. They say, 'Wow!' just like you did. And now, my friend, they're getting filled with hope and belief."

I was writing furiously.

"And here's what happens next. They see results, which they like. And they already know what the actions are that they're taught in the system. They read, they listen, they associate with growing people, and they share. They are getting clear on the <u>Action Steps</u> that they need to do if they want to get the kind of results that lead to success.

"Right?"

I nodded.

"But they don't know how much to do. How many plans should they show if they want to make fast progress? How many books should they read to get their own mind regeared for success? How may audios should they listen to in order to get all the failure talk burned out of their soul and new thoughts and life-changing information into their hearts and minds?"

I was loving it. I'm a salesman. I'm all about metrics. You want something to happen, you've got to measure it. You want a certain result, you need to know how much to invest to get that result.

"You know that I've managed salespeople, right, Bradford?" I interjected.

"Absolutely!"

"And I know that you know what happens. If you don't teach your people what success requires, some don't work hard enough, and some don't know when to quit."

"It's a problem either way, Bobby," Bradford jumped right back in. "Some you hire look great on paper, but they skimp on the discipline end. They don't do the necessary daily behaviors. And then they don't understand why they aren't getting superstar results."

"And," I took back over, "some you hire screw up their marriages by never leaving work. They can't say when enough is enough."

I smiled. I was sure Bradford knew exactly who I was talking about right there.

"So in <u>Action Step 4: Move the Train</u>, we quantify it. We know what success requires, so we teach it."

"It's part of the system," I threw in. I was getting this! And I loved it!

Bradford laughed.

"I already told you about our Club 180°, Bobby," he plowed on. "And I promised to show you how to build this into a self-management tool that you can track every day. I'm sending you a worksheet right now. Look for it in your email. This is a monthly worksheet. Turn your life around by reading, listening, associating with good people, and sharing this compensated community with others. Accumulate 180 points each month, and you'll be on your way to changing your thinking to change your life."

My inbox dinged, and I opened up the attachment. "I've got it."

"Look down the left-hand side, Bobby. It says '# of PLANS,' and it's got about twenty or so lines."

It looked like this:

Club 180°

Name: _____   Month: _____

The **Club 180°** program is designed to help the PRIMARY PLAN SHOWER create the
vital behaviors for success. Each month, set the goal to reach 180 degrees.
You receive 1 degree for each audio you listen to and 6 degrees for each plan you
show. Reach 180 degrees through any combination of audios and plans.
For example, 3 audios a day over 30 days = 90 degrees. 15 plans x 6
degrees each = 90 degrees. Combined, that equals 180 degrees!

of PLANS

	Date	Name
1		
2		
3		
4		
5		
6		
7		
8		
9		
10		
11		
12		
13		
14		
15		
16		
17		
18		
19		
20		

"True learning occurs when people listen to
audios to gain knowledge and then apply it!"
– *Orrin Woodward*

of AUDIOS

*In the spaces provided below, write down the
number of audios you listen to each day this month.*

1	2	3	4	5	6	7
8	9	10	11	12	13	14
15	16	17	18	19	20	21
22	23	24	25	26	27	28
29	30	31				

☐ **READ AT LEAST ONE BOOK**

☑ **BONUS DEGREES!**

*For your first month of **Club 180°** ONLY, you can
earn 30 extra bonus degrees! Earn 6 degrees for
each Tuesday Open Meeting and 6 degrees for
attending your local Monthly Seminar!**

☐ I attended my 1st Open Meeting
☐ I attended my 2nd Open Meeting
☐ I attended my 3rd Open Meeting
☐ I attended my 4th Open Meeting
☐ I attended my Monthly Seminar

FINAL SCORE

\# of Plan degrees: _____
\# of Audio degrees: _____
\# of Bonus degrees: _____

TOTAL DEGREES: _____

* The number of Opens may vary from month to month depending on the calendar and holidays.

"And down the right-hand side, it says '# of AUDIOS'
and has about thirty-five or so spaces to track them. And
then it has a spot to mark whether you've read at least one
book that month."

I saw.

"And at the bottom is a 'FINAL SCORE' section where you tally your 'TOTAL DEGREES' for the month."

I saw it all.

"So read at least one book a month, and check the box. And every time you show a plan, fill in one of the plan lines with the date and who you showed it to, and then score the points. And every time you listen to an audio, putting good information into your head and driving out the defeatist noise, write down the one you listened to, and score the points. Every month, accumulate 180 points. That's the score to hit, and you'll fly to the moon."

"Give me the quick math, Bradford," I inquired. "What's a simple way to get to 180 points?"

"Fifteen plans a month, Bobby, one book a month, and three audios a day. Those are your behaviors in 'Move the Train.' Do them and teach everybody in your team to do them, and you'll be unstoppable!"

"Why is listening to an audio a behavior?" I asked, but I knew before I had the question out what the answer was.

"Because our whole business is about growing people, Bobby! We talked about this in Michigan. You've got to get the limiting beliefs out of your head and replace them with empowering ones. I think of this as 'Truth Coffee.' I can't put any more 'Truth Coffee' into your cup if your cup doesn't have the capacity to hold it! The books and audios increase your capacity — and the capacity of the people on your team. And at the end of the day, it's *people* who build our business! So we are in the business of building our people to build our business."

I did get it! I got it. Well, it's probably more accurate to say that I was getting it. And I needed this: I needed to be grown, to be invested in, to get new information and messages into my head, just as much as I needed oxygen to breathe and water to drink. My life, my future, everything I hoped for was riding on it.

Bradford and I wrapped up around 9:30 in the morning. I had a good group ready to come to my house at 6:30 later in the evening. It had seemed like a complete day, so far as tonight was concerned. I had planned to start making calls to set things up for next week. But Bradford had just blown my mind.

I jumped on the phone and made three very important phone calls. I called three of the people that I had seen during the week who had wanted to talk further. We already had tentative agreements to sit down on Saturday or early next week and follow through.

But the world had shifted, and I knew that with some effort and also with some good fortune, I could catch up with one or more of them still today. And understanding what I now understood, I knew that I needed to get them to see that what we would do at our meeting that night would benefit them, since I had shown the plan to them first. Therefore, when I followed up with them next week, they could already have people ready to get started underneath them with customer volume flowing. I was really catching onto this Team Approach concept!

For them, whether they came to tonight's meeting or not, it still mattered. My follow-throughs next week would prove to them that I was serious about building a compensated community because I would share the results of tonight's meeting with them and explain how they could benefit if they go ahead and hold their spot on the train. We truly are in business *for* ourselves but not *by* ourselves.

And it would matter for the Ruscittos, the Painters, and Bill and Barbara—not to mention three other couples that I didn't personally know. I already had the awesome news to share tonight with my teammates that three additional couples had come onto their teams. I was suddenly very hungry to keep this momentum going to blow the minds of everyone in my community.

As my mind had just been blown.

To build their belief.

Just like mine.

CHAPTER 9

ACTION STEP 5: LAY TRAIN TRACKS

I must begin with an apology. The last words that I wrote ("To build their belief. Just like mine.") were written just over four months ago. I intended to keep writing in this journal, if not every day, then every few days for sure. I planned to keep a very close log of my activities, of what I was learning, and of the rawness of it all.

I wanted to get it all down on paper.

But I wrote those words on a Friday morning right after hanging up the phone with Bradford Henderson. I think of that day as the day it all clicked. I should say *kaboomed*! That explosive day was two weeks out from my shopping cart collision with Bradford in the Kroger of downtown Davison, Michigan. In those two weeks, he had taught me a lot of things, including the principle he called "Move the Train." But then he showed me what he actually meant by "Move the Train" by adding people to my team. Bradford and Don and Doris physically moved my train! And boy did I feel it move!

The sonic blast of seeing that this company was the real deal transformed the fire of my determination into an absolute conflagration. And I've been a brightly lit torch of full-on engagement ever since.

Let me fill you in on a few details.

I was successful on that Friday. You recall that I had three couples pretty much ready to Get On the Train. I had planned to follow through with them over that next several days, but Bradford's phone call made my messaging for follow-throughs so much easier. I signed up all three couples when we got together by simply reporting to them how well the Friday night meeting had gone. When they realized that all the new people would be in their group if they held their spot, it was like catching fish from a barrel. In all fairness, however, I (well, Bradford) had shown them the plan first, and I had told them any work I did after talking to them would be part of their group if they chose to join. This is how Team Approach works. We win as a team. Friday night's meeting was the team's way of working for the people we talked to the week before.

About that Friday night meeting, the Ruscittos, Painters, Baxters, and I were pumped when I checked the LIFE Leadership site and realized another new person had been added to our team by someone in our support team. My newest colleagues were feeling the "wow" that I had so articulately expressed to Bradford when I first felt it.

The train was moving!

Wow!

That evening was awesome! Don and Doris led the presentation of the plan for the guests, answered questions, helped me and my partners walk our guests through the steps, modeled how the system works, and reinforced that we always follow the system. And then I took all my business partners out for a late-evening dessert afterward.

"The train is moving ahead because we are working together as a *team*," I said to them at the restaurant. "Individuals grow, but teams explode, and we are *exploding*. Thankfully, we have a system. If we follow the leaders with proven results and do what they do, then it will work for us like it worked for them. Those who dream and do consistently produce the biggest results. We're building a business here, and that means producing consistent, repeatable, and powerful growth. Just as a McDonald's owner follows a proven system, we follow a proven system. Learn to let the business system do the work!"

Well, so that was Friday. The next day, we were in follow-through mode. Phone calls were flying back and forth between us. It felt so good to be working together as a tightly orchestrated team. Everybody was excited. I kept driving for results, following up with people who had come to see the plan, and making new calls to set up my following week of presenting the plan to newcomers. I used the Club 180° reporting framework to pace myself and put this into each of my teammate's hands as well. I listened to audios as I drove from appointment to appointment. I was energized!

I also thought a lot about Pam and my children that Saturday. They were going to be home the very next day. And I was nervous, excited, and scared.

And, well, they came home. And that was that, so far as this little journal is concerned.

My solitude ended on that Sunday. There were no more late-night, lonely soul-searching sessions. No more "what am I going to do with myself" conundrums after the rest of the world was asleep and I wasn't sleepy. No more "at least I've got my journal to entertain me!"

Pam and my kids tumbled off the Jetway Sunday late afternoon, and my life became instantly noisy and full. I hauled them straight away from the airport directly to a waffle and ice cream parlor. "Serve cookies and cream" was a business principle, to be sure, but the reason it works in business, I now know, is that it is a principle that is rooted in life itself.

Sitting crammed into a big booth, waffles, ice cream, fudge, strawberry sauce, and whipped cream splattered over everything, I listened to my three kids narrate their two weeks in Michigan at full stereophonic volume. And all the while that I listened, I observed Pam quietly and lovingly observing me. My ears were busy taking in the voices of my beautiful children. My eyes moved back and forth from child to Pam to child to Pam to child and back to Pam.

Simply stated, I never thought about my journal again—not until today. And as I've already said, I'm sorry about that.

I think you can understand that I'm also *not* sorry! Yes, I'm sorry that I didn't write more, but I'm not sorry about *why*.

As I write this, Pam and the kids are in Cozumel. They're doing a two-week unit on the Mayan Indians, and, well, homeschooling does have its perks. We decided that we could all use a change of scenery here in late April. They headed out three days ago; I'll be joining them tomorrow.

Notice the pattern? Pam and the kids are gone. And, voilà, I'm once again a journaler! You'd better enjoy this while it lasts!

Obviously, there's more to the story than what I've gotten down in these few extra pages. So let me fill you in.

I went from being an employee and a manager of a small sales team to being the captain of a new enterprise that was going to be as big as I was willing to dream. And it's not like I decided that I wanted a huge organization for the sake of having a huge organization. It's rather that everybody I brought into my organization deserved, in my estimation, to be as successful as they wanted to be. Their success required their growth. Their growth needed my guidance and support. If they were to grow, I needed to invest in them, to help them bring in others who them-selves deserved to be successful. The size of my organiza-tion wasn't the product of my ambition for myself; it was the product of my dedication to the success of each person that I had the privilege of inviting onto my team.

And what has fueled and sustained me to get from where I was to where I am? Obviously, that's a question with a lot of dimensions to it, but let me give you the true, elegant, and simple answer: I've been disciplined about the books I read, the audios I listen to, and the people I hang around with. I took Bradford seriously when he showed me Club 180°, and I've been following it. And equally important, I teach every member of my organization the same thing. "Your success is directly related to how many people are learning, growing, and being inspired when you are not around." That's what I teach. It's what I practice. This simple discipline — reading, listening, and spending my time with positive, fruitful people — is what makes this business so much more than a business, and it has given me a new way of looking at things, which changes how I behave, day by day.

And, well, when you follow this discipline — the Club 180° blueprint — and you learn to look at things in a better way, the sky becomes the limit. In fact, it has become clear to me that no other way of looking at things would be fair to the people I am serving.

Another way to say this is that I decided that I would be the person who chose just how quickly I got promoted. My pay raise would become effective as soon as I became effective. It was *my* responsibility.

It makes me laugh to think about how shocked I was when I heard Bradford talking this way. It seemed crazy at first to believe that I was the only person who could limit my climbing the ladder of success. After all, this wasn't the way it worked in my corporate environment. I now know that there isn't anything more realistic and less selfish in the world than the commitment to grow as rapidly as your service to others demands. That being the case, I decided that I'd put myself on the fastest track possible!

And then what happened?

Well, what happened then is that I got myself into a ton of trouble. Bradford had told me there was one more Action Step, and boy was he right.

There's an old saying that "nothing breeds failure quite like success!" Fortunately, Bradford understood this just as the founders of LIFE Leadership did. They designed a system—yes, there it is again, a SYSTEM—to handle the crisis of growth and success, or I'd have gone the way of lots of flash-in-the-pan wonder boys. Like Kiyosaki says, "The world is full of smart broke people!"[1] If Bradford hadn't given me the rest of their training program, I'd have become one more of Kiyosaki's smart paupers— smart, *exhausted* paupers, to be more precise!

So all that is to say that a business needs to have systems in place that can handle great growth. Otherwise, what's the point? If growth isn't the point and if being able to handle great growth without being crushed isn't the point, then I may as well just go back to selling my time for money.

What I hadn't yet learned, back at the point when things really exploded, was that the most important system of all is the system—hang on to your hats here!—that enables your business to grow beyond your capacity to grow your business. When we are no longer competent to handle the level of success we have achieved, which is what we hope will happen, then the business system must be competent enough to do what we aren't competent to do. Did I lose you there? Well, if I did lose you, then welcome to the club because I came within an inch of losing myself over this well-worn paradox.

In short, here's what happened.

I worked the system. Having done <u>Action Step 1: Get On the Train</u>, I immediately set about the work of <u>Action Step 2: Get Others onto the Train</u>. "Hold your spot," I told them. "Jump on board! This train is going places!"

Then, I worked <u>Action Step 3: Serve Cookies and Cream</u>. Every single one of my new partners was a valuable human being. They all deserved love, respect, genuine personal attention, and care. And I gave it to them. I had no idea which ones would actually do the work that success required. We already covered this point in the previous pages. I'm not God. Who am I to tag somebody out? Given the fact that I should have been tagged out myself—by Bradford, of course, but more fundamentally by Pam—I wasn't going to turn around and be a jerk about the hopes and dreams others had for themselves! I signed them up if they aspired to be signed up, and I cared the living daylights out of them!

And then—oh boy!—I did <u>Action Step 4: Move the Train</u>. Well, Bradford did <u>Action Step 4</u> for me, and when he put all that momentum inside of me through his actions, I had the momentum to pass on to others. You can't give what you don't have! I was given it, and so I had it to give.

And on that second Friday in December, I watched the beginning of my great success. Growth was exciting and explosive! What I *didn't* know on that day was that I was also planting the seeds of my failure.

I didn't know it. But Bradford did.

"Son of a gun, Bobby!" Bradford had crowed when I called him for our monthly mentoring session. We typically talked live once or twice per month after that first couple of weeks when I learned the science side (techniques) of the business. And Bradford continued teaching me the art side (leadership). He studied his online business reports daily, so I knew he knew how I was doing.

"You're tearing it up!" he continued. "I'm looking at your achievements, and you're climbing the *Next Step* "Ladder to Success" about as fast as it has ever been done. That was a statement, but I also sensed there was a question somewhere inside it.

"Thanks, Bradford," I chuckled. I also let out a sigh. I *was* burning it up. Or was it me who was getting burned up? "I'm having the time of my life," I added. I was! I was having the time of my life. And I was also getting burned up.

"So, Bobby," Bradford went on, "I have studied your business data, and I know you blew through achieving Power Player last December and have broken a Leader rank in one leg and a Student 10,000 in another. Man, you have an outside shot of hitting Coordinator before the next major convention. Way to go!" he added.

The line went silent for a second, and I waited.

"That's what I can see. Tell me about what I can't see. How are *you* and the family doing?"

"We're good," I answered quickly—too quickly. The fact of the matter was that we were good. Truly! Come on! I was working my butt off proving that this wasn't another famous Bobby train wreck. I had quit being a quitter! And I was out to prove it.

And Pam's strong approval of me was unwavering, though to be honest, I was seeing the beginnings of a question mark on her face as she watched me work. I'm no Einstein, but I knew pretty much exactly what the question mark was aimed at.

"We're good," I repeated. "But I'm sure you know what kind of hours we've been logging to build our business as fast as we've been building it. Pam and I have loved the reading, listening, and associating steps, but we have stretched ourselves pretty thin with my job, our family, and our new fast-growing business."

"I see. Frankly, that's what especially stands out to me. You've got a boatload of Power Players on your team already! None of them went Power Player without you giving them extraordinary time and support. Trust me," he continued. "I know what I'm looking at here. I've done it, and I know what you're doing. I'm impressed, Bobby."

Another pause.

"And I'm also concerned."

"Can I be honest with you, Bradford?" I then asked. I was suddenly in a very subdued mood. Bradford was my friend. I knew that he loved me. We were way past pretenses. I could be myself with him.

"Every week has given me and my teammates growth and success," I pressed on. I didn't wait for him to give me permission to be honest, as I didn't need him to even answer that question, and he knew I didn't.

"We're seeing incredible growth. Pam and I are thrilled, and my teammates are thrilled. But every new partner that we add to our team makes our workload just that much greater.

"Honestly, Bradford," I emphatically added, "I don't know if I can survive much more success!"

Bradford laughed. It was a big, relieved, fellow traveler's laugh, the kind of laugh when you're laughing *with* someone—when you personally understand the malady that's being described to you, you're relieved that your buddy is being candid about his struggles, you've got a bad case of that same struggle yourself, and you love having true friends on the journey with you.

"Bobby, you have slammed into one of the toughest leadership challenges that confronts a new leader: exponential growth. And you got there even faster than I did!"

I didn't say anything. I was smiling. And I was shaking my head. It really felt good to be on the phone with my friend.

"And the leadership growth challenge you've slammed into is not easy to navigate, which is why most leaders end their journey here. In fact, without a systematic leadership plan to develop other leaders, you won't get through this one either," Bradford continued, "because you simply cannot manufacture any more hours in a day, which is why the LIFE Leadership founders built a leadership development system to help you and everybody else in the company break through this Goliath!

"You wanna know what it is?" he continued.

"I'm all ears, Bradford."

"Write this down: 'You can't be everything to everybody!'"

"But you said that I should serve my people cookies and cream and move their train!" I retorted. I wasn't arguing. I knew for darn certain that he had an answer to my challenge, but I was confused.

"And I'm sure you've shared with them and their people that their job is to serve cookies and cream to *their* people and move the train for them, too," Bradford replied.

True. I had.

"And are they doing it?"

"They are." The tone of my voice wasn't particularly convincing.

"But?" Bradford pressed.

"But the people we're bringing in today would really like to hear from me also," I answered. "I'm no egomaniac, and saying that made me feel uncomfortable. But it really blesses the socks off of the new folks to get a personal touch from the guy they see as their 'superhero.' Or perhaps it is that they intuitively know that I am, in fact, **not** a superhero but just as regular as they are yet still making it. In either case, when I give personal attention to newcomers, it produces pretty spectacular results. People feel dignified. Encouraged."

"And what are you going to do about that once you've got *twice* as many people as you currently have?" Bradford challenged.

"How about ten times the people?" he pressed further.

"A thousand times the people?" he threw on top. He was burying my arguments, and he had every intention of doing so.

"Die," was all I could think of answering.

Bradford laughed again—loudly!

"Chrissie and the kids and I are in Florida through mid-June," Bradford interjected. "Get over here! Can you? You and the family?" he added. "Let's talk this through!"

*　　　*　　　*　　　*

Not too long after that, Pam and the kids and I flew to Florida, moved into Bradford and Chrissie's carriage house for a long weekend, had the time of our lives lounging along the waterfront, and laughed more than we've laughed in several years. Chrissie and Pam hung out. Our kids and their kids had a great time together. And Bradford finished giving me my training program. That is to say, he finished giving me his hands-on training secrets, which I'm now giving to you.

I'm the most blessed man on earth! And it is my hope that my good fortune, through this little journal, becomes your good fortune, too.

Why am I getting all of this down on paper? Why, when Pam and my kids are traipsing around Mayan pyramids in Cozumel, am I sitting here, late into the night, writing down what happened to me? I'm doing it because I want you to get the benefit. My life isn't about me! My life is about how my life can be useful to your life. The value of my life won't be measured in terms of the visible achievements of my life. The value of my life will be measured in terms of the use I am to your life. Bradford believes this about himself. I believe this about myself.

And I recommend that you start believing this about yourself.

It's not about you!

Now let's make our lives count for others!

You with me?

"<u>Action Step 5: Lay Train Tracks!</u>"

Bradford nearly shouted these words—not that he needed to. I was sitting in his "library" in his Florida home. It looked like a fourteenth-century monastic library in some Italianate structure of antiquity. The bookcases stood ten feet tall in a round, Romanesque edifice, with small windows rimming the perimeter above the books. The roof of this library was an octagonal turret, with beautiful beams rising to a shared center from each of the eight corners.

Pam and my kids were out on some romp with Chrissie and their kids. I wasn't even sure where they were. This was the last of the foundational business lessons that Bradford taught to all of his top up-and-coming leaders, and I had my pen and paper at the ready.

Bradford looked me straight in the eye and stated, "The key to a long-term, sustainable, and duplicatable compensated community is to learn to lay new train tracks so others can learn to drive their own trains. As you develop more leaders who can drive their own trains on the tracks you have laid for them, the bigger your results will be in your organization. And the results will be produced without everything being dependent upon your time and skill in driving trains. You simply run out of time if you attempt to drive every train; however, your results become practically unlimited when you learn to lay tracks for others and teach them how to drive their own trains. In other words, leverage yourself."

"Leverage?" I questioned.

"Archimedes once said, 'Give me a lever long enough and a fulcrum on which to place it, and I shall move the world.'[2] Similar to Archimedes' idea of using physical leverage to multiply his power to move the world, leadership leverage multiplies your influence within your community. You, Bobby, like all leaders, have natural ways to touch people on your team," Bradford pressed on. "You'll see them at the Tuesday meetings, and you'll greet them as friends, learn and remember their names, and shower love on them."

I was already doing that.

"And you'll spend time with everybody at regional events, at our national major functions, and so forth. You need to understand who you are in their eyes! You're their big brother, their hero, the one who's gone ahead. They all want to know that you care for them!"

No confusion on this point.

"Okay, Bradford," I interjected, "I can see this so far as the Tuesday Open Meetings, the Monthly Seminars, and the Leadership Conventions are concerned. I love the energy of these events and can pour love and encouragement into people with no problem at those meetings. After all, if people are committed to be at our key business gatherings, I know they're serious about this business!"

Bradford smiled and nodded his head emphatically. We were on the same page, as far as this went.

"The question, Bobby, is how available you are during the rest of your week—how available and to whom."

"Say more," was all I could come up with in response to this.

"If you want big growth, if you want to 'move the world' by leveraging your leadership beyond any single leader's capacity, then you've got to rely on the distinctions that naturally develop in all communities. Since a leader's most valuable resource is his time, you must let the performance of individuals on your team determine who you should invest extra time with. You can't be everything to everybody, or you will end up being nothing to no one!"

"So who do you want to be somebody to?" Bradford continued.

I stared off into space. It wasn't that I wasn't listening. I was thinking.

"Okay," I began. Then I went silent for another few moments.

"I can give cookies and cream to lots of people at our Open Meetings, seminars, and major conventions. I can gear up for those, be there, lay myself aside, and pour everything I've got into loving, being with, encouraging, and affirming people in my organization."

I was thinking out loud.

And Bradford just kept nodding his head. He understood my process.

"But if my company is ten times — or a thousand times — bigger than it is now, well then, I'm out of time," I added.

Call me Captain Obvious!

"And your kids and Pam are right back at square one with you," Bradford threw in.

Indeed!

"So your question is: Who do I want to be somebody extra to? May I elaborate on your question, Bradford?" I asked.

He nodded once.

"In addition to what I'll do for everybody, which is love and honor them, who do I want to give extra, additional mentorship time to?"

"Right! Exactly!"

"I want to give extra mentorship time to those who are doing what it takes to win," I answered, sure that my answer was Bradford's answer. "I don't know who will do what it takes, at least not when I sign them up. However, I'll know soon enough who actually *is* doing it, not by what they say but by what they do. And I'll want to give them a very clear message that I see what they're doing and that I'm there to help them."

"Why?" Bradford "Socrates" Henderson had apparently decided to make a trip from Greece to Italy in order to hang out in this glorious library!

"Because the people who are doing the work and learning to lead can most effectively help me influence the rest of the community toward our goals and game plans. I invest in the top leaders within my community, and they invest into hundreds of others, freeing up my time through the power of leverage. They can leverage my leadership into their teams without me having to do it all. If I invest my time in teaching them, they can invest their time in serving their communities more effectively, and the resulting leverage frees up the leader's time. This is the definition of a true 'B' business."

"And what, Bobby, is the greatest resource you have to offer the people in your organization who are doing what success demands?"

"Myself!" At the end of the day, offering myself was the best I had.

True for Pam.

True for my kids.

True for my business colleagues.

I would leverage myself, providing mentoring to those who are building their leadership capacities by doing what it takes to win. I would do this because these are the people who will immediately apply the lessons learned, multiplying and, eventually, exponentially growing their business. We would build a leadership culture within our organization that rewards performance. Everybody would be loved, but the key performers—who themselves would be serving cookies and cream to their team—would get the most mentorship time since they would leverage leadership into the group to multiply the results for all.

"There's a paradox here, too," Bradford added. "If you give equal time to everybody, then everyone suffers. The leaders in the group do not have their leadership cups filled, while the rest have "Truth Coffee" spilling over their filled capacities. Remember, leaders in a free market system always rise to the top. If you invest your time with your top performers and teach them to do the same thing with their best performers, everybody in the community benefits through better results, encouragement, and focus. In short, leaders feed the performers, who feed the new people getting started.

"It's a multiplication process," he added. "And it's your job as leader to be smart enough, loving enough, and courageous enough to leverage yourself to drive the greatest good, the greatest love, and the greatest productivity into your community. Instead of meeting with everyone on your team after an Open, maybe it's time to start meeting with the Club 180° Go-Getters (those who have fulfilled Club 180° and shown fifteen plans per month. Or in your bigger teams, maybe it's time to start mentoring just your CAB (Community Advancement Bonus) qualifiers. Distinction drives who to sit down with because it keeps politics (who you like or who you think is going to do it) out of the process and instead keeps it centered on current efforts and results. Otherwise, you will exhaust yourself because your community has become too big for you to do all the servant leadership needed. Thankfully, you now are in a position to teach your top leaders how to serve the way you do through the power of leverage—laying train tracks."

"And teach them to lay train tracks also!" I enthusiastically added.

The smile on Bradford's face was as big as a sunrise!

"Laying train tracks is how we leverage our results to reach millions of people with life-changing leadership information."

CHAPTER 10

RIGHT WALL, RIGHT LADDER

I started writing in this journal at a point in my life when I was in a hole. Okay, it was bigger than a hole. I was in a cavern. I was in a Grand Canyon–sized cavern. In a fantastical gorge, a bottomless ravine, a defile. If you can come up with a word that describes a super-gigunda chasm that's bigger than the words I thought of putting in that last sentence, then knock yourself out!

I was low, okay?

The least important part of the hole that I was in was the job part. True enough, I was super unhappy with my job. I had tried for over a decade to be cool with the fact that I was pretty well rewarded for doing stuff that other people told me to do. But I wasn't cool with it, and I had driven Pam, my beloved wife, nearly to despair with my adolescent outbursts about it.

What do I mean by "adolescent outbursts"? What I mean is that I didn't take charge of my unhappiness. I didn't take charge of me. I postured as the sad, unappreciated artiste, the virtuous victim, the justifiably angst-ridden innocent who was "done to." God, the universe, the man, my boss—they all "did it to me"! And who could blame poor, pathetic me? At the end of the day, I wasn't to blame. Wasn't at fault. Wasn't guilty for my sorry state. Wasn't responsible.

Which is another way of saying that I wasn't grown-up.

That's what I mean by "adolescent outbursts." I behaved like a child in a man's body.

Henry David Thoreau said, "The mass of men lead lives of quiet desperation."[1] I understood this first-hand. And Benjamin Franklin said, "Some people die at 25 and aren't buried until 75."[2] You can tell I have been listening to audios, huh? Without a doubt, I was one of the walking dead!

Frankly, it made me sick to my stomach.

And I can hardly imagine how it felt to be my wife. She had bargained for a marriage with a man. Instead, she got to watch her husband whine away his existence in an adolescent tantrum. That's never what a strong woman bargains for. A strong woman bargains for a partnership with a strong man. That's the deal she's looking for.

Am I being too hard on myself?

I don't think so. A man, first and foremost, is willing to take a full punch straight to the chin. They say the truth will set you free, but for me that's only true after it ticks me off. I'm not being too hard on myself because I wanted to be a man. If truth is what I need, then bring it on!

Fact is, my friends, there comes a time when we realize that it's time to grow up. Man up. Stand up.

When I started this journal, I hadn't reached that particular point in time. I hadn't yet manned up.

The far more important part of the hole that I was in was the marriage part. Pam had been doing (well, let's just be a little generous with me right here) more than 50 percent of the marriage work. Shall we give her 51 percent and me 49 percent? Being generous!

I wouldn't protest if you thought that Pam was giving 99.9 percent and me the remainder of the 100 percent.

And I don't even know how to begin to talk about my amazing kids. They didn't ask to be conceived. They didn't ask to be ushered, screaming if not also kicking, into this world. But Pam and I hauled them on over from the mind of God into their earthly travail, no vote given to them in the deal, and then I proceeded to largely ignore them. I largely ignored them, that is, right up until this journal started.

I say that the far more important part of the hole that I was in when I started this journal was the marriage part, but it's more complete to say that it was the family part. I was in the truly big hole, in the hole that mattered, with my family. My responsibility as husband and father far out-ranked my responsibility as employee, worker, breadwinner, entrepreneur, or business owner. It was as a husband and father that I had really laid an egg!

When I look at the big picture, I'm ashamed. The place where I most needed change was in that family place — in my place as husband and dad.

But what got me actually motivated was my job life. This is what shames me. Wouldn't you think that I'd get motivated by problems in my family life? I'd be *proud* to say that my devotion to my family is what got me motivated. But that's not how it happened, as you've seen.

What got me motivated, actually, was bumping my shopping cart into Bradford Henderson, seeing that he was doing fantastically well in his job life, and then feeling awful about myself.

This is what embarrasses me.

But then again, when I look at the *really* big picture, I'm amazed even more than I'm embarrassed. So it's true that I got motivated by petty issues. I got motivated by work frustrations and by making ridiculous comparisons between how I was doing at work and how my friend Bradford was doing with his work. This is sick! There's no world-class virtue in this admission, let me tell you.

And yet, as I got to work with Bradford and as Pam and I got reconnected with Bradford and Chrissie, the more important issues of my life and of our family life came into focus. Yes, I worked on my job life, but in the course of doing so, I got to work on my *life* life, too — on my true life, on the things of my life that mattered more.

My son, Rob, is in love. I think I intimated as much. He turned sixteen in January, and he's having a wonderful time here in Mexico, but his heart is in Michigan. "Rob,"

I said to him last night, "it's April, and it's still snowing in Michigan. Why are you thinking about cold Michigan when you are basking in the sun here?"

"Robert!" That was Pam, giving me the warning intonation, the twinkling eye, and the raised eyebrow that my banter deserved.

Rob just smiled, ear to ear, blushing. He was guilty as charged! All he was thinking about was a very sunny girl who was 1,583 miles away in frigid Davison, Michigan. He was thinking about her, and the fact that she was suffering another blast of the so-called Arctic Vortex didn't change the fact that the thought of her made his heart feel warmer than Mexico.

My children have changed. Simply, they've noticed that I'm with them. Their communications are no longer tentative, guarded, and uncertain as to whether I'll notice that they're trying to communicate with me. Now, their communications are just communications, gestures and pranks and jokes and musings that they offer up with confidence that I'm with them. That I'm paying attention. That I wouldn't for the world miss what they're playing around with. And though they're always playing around, they're never just playing around. Rather, they're always testing, reaching out, trying things, and looking for response.

Looking for *my* response.

More fundamentally, looking for my notice.

Am I noticing them, they are wondering. Am I with them? Do I care?

The answer is I am. I do.

I'm no longer in a hole.

Rather, I'm in my life. I'm no more perfect than I was. No more competent. No more in control.

What I am, rather, is present. Connected. Aware. Conscious. Appreciative. With.

The other thing that I should point out is that I started writing in this journal at a point when the ladder of my life was leaning up against the wrong wall. Well, that's at least how I thought about it at the time.

I thought of my life as a problem. The problem was that I needed to get somewhere. So I guess you could say that I thought of my life as a problem of needing to get somewhere.

And since my life was a problem, and the problem was that I needed to get somewhere—and it goes without saying that I wasn't where I needed to get to—then the need I had was to learn where I should go and how I should get there. I'm no genius, as I've amply documented in this journal. But that sums my problem up pretty comprehensively, don't you think?

Come on! Let's get real! I wasn't where I needed to be, and my life was a problem; therefore, the solution to my problem—to my life—would be found in figuring out where I needed to be and how I needed to get there.

In short, I needed everything: a starting line, a map to the finish line, a way to get from the starting line to the finish line, and the navigational competency to do what the map said.

Or if I can shorthand this, it was less that I needed everything as it was that I was *lost*.

When I started writing in this journal, I was lost with no compass.

Wasn't that what you were actually thinking about me, back at the start?

Be honest!

A little while ago, I said that I was embarrassed. Then I said that I was amazed. Let me wrap this up by saying that I am very, very thankful.

Pam and my kids are on a zip-line adventure today. We spent two hours early this morning touching base with each other. I asked each of us to answer this question: "What is present in your life today that *didn't* used to be that allows you to give yourself 100 percent to what today will bring?"

What we said to each other this morning was priceless. Beautiful. Very encouraging.

I told my family about my commitment to you, the reader of this journal. I told them that I had nearly finished my notes to you. That I promised myself that I'd put everything Bradford gave me into a journal that you could use to benefit your life in the same way that he benefited mine. I told them I was just a few pages away from being done with this duty, the duty I feel toward you.

I then asked them if they'd be willing to excuse me from the zip-line adventure. And I promised them I'd be full-on with them tomorrow.

So I think you're getting what I'm doing now. I'm wrapping this journal up. I'm fulfilling the promise I made to myself to take everything Bradford gave me and turn it into a gift to you.

Way back at the beginning of this journal, Bradford talked with me about a ladder. He said he felt that he had leaned the ladder of his life against the wrong wall. And I felt exactly the same way. I didn't trust that my career ladder was taking me to a destination that I even wanted to go.

In that same conversation, Bradford spouted some incomprehensible nonsense about looking for a wall that was so tall that he could lean the ladder of his life against it and know that the height of the wall couldn't possibly dampen his ambition — or something like that. Bradford wanted to lean his ladder against a wall that could take him anywhere, and that's why he shocked our coworkers back then by walking away from a very promising career ladder.

Here's what I know now.

The ladder is nothing more than the vehicle I choose to travel in on my life's journey.

The wall that I'm leaning my ladder against is nothing more than my purpose in life.

It's my ladder. It's my wall.

That's it.

I'm living my life.

I'm with Pam and with my kids.

I'm doing my work.

I get up in the morning, and whatever happens that day is what gives me my opportunities to learn, to serve, and to grow.

No one owes me anything.

And I get gifts and help and surprises and grace and blessings from the four corners of the world. What I'm not saying is that I make everything happen. Many things happen as a result of the team, of the community of colleagues—those in my support team and those that I support. I'm a part of a "we." And it's "we" who are doing all the great work.

So no one owes me anything, but many people have contributed pricelessly to me.

And it is my prayer that I contribute pricelessly to many.

It's my ladder and wall. But this community—what Bradford calls the 'compensated community'—is the house that my wall belongs to. I decide what I will do each day. But many others alter the equation of what I decide by bringing their gifts forward for the purpose of building our shared house.

In short, I'm free.

I belong to others.

I'm responsible.

I'm helped every day by hundreds and thousands of others.

I'm committed.

My life, at its best, is a gift to others, a gift even to people I may never meet.

I used to never know where to start. I told you that. I didn't know where to start, how to start, or when to start. That's what I wrote in my first few pages of this journal.

And that has all changed. Thanks to what I learned, I know where to start, how to start, and when to start. I know it just as clearly as I know who I am and to whom I belong.

May I help you with this part, too? Yes, I know it goes beyond passing along the Action Steps Bradford gave me, but the Action Steps depend on the understandings I'm about to share.

Where should you start?

You should start exactly where you are. It's a wonderful place to start, precisely because it's where you are. You alone are qualified to start there.

How should you start?

You should start by getting brutally clear with yourself that your life isn't about you. Your life is about others. You live to serve. How should you start? You should start by asking yourself, "How can I make a difference today?" Answer that question, and then get to it!

When should you start?

May I propose now? Is there anything wrong with starting now? Do a gut check, please! Ask yourself, "How does *now* feel?" If now feels right to you, then why don't you make the decision here and now — the decision to "sign up and hold your spot" in the eternal business of life — and then get to it. Life is waiting! Your service is needed. You're the only one who happens to occupy the place that you occupy. Who better to be you than you, after all, and to be the person who goes ahead and gets to work right away, serving right there in the place where you find yourself?

Would you like to get on the leadership train?

NOTES

Chapter 3: U-Turn

1 Unknown, often attributed to Albert Einstein. See icarus-falling. blogspot.ca/2009/06/Einstein-enigma.html.

Chapter 4: Action Step 1: Get On the Train

1 The Nielsen Company, "Consumer Trust in Online, Social and Mobile Advertising Grows," 04-10-2012, copyright 2014 The Nielsen Company, http://www.nielsen.com/us/en/insights/news/2012/consumer-trust-in-online-social-and-mobile-advertising-grows.html.

2 Stephen R. Covey, *The 7 Habits of Highly Effective People: Powerful Lessons in Personal Change, 25th Anniversary Edition* (New York: Simon & Schuster, 2013), p. 217.

3 Tom Peters, *The Circle of Innovation: You Can't Shrink Your Way to Greatness* (New York: Vintage Books, 1999).

4 Tom Peters, quoting Al McDonald, former Managing Director of McKinsey & Co, as saying, "Never forget implementation, boys. In our work, it's what I call the 'last 98 percent' of the client puzzle" to a project team that included Tom Peters, reported by subsequent McKinsey MD, Ron Daniel, tompeters.com/slides/uploaded/implementation_Mstr_041708_web.ppt, tompeters.com/slides/uploaded/ACTThinkDoPSFWOWGrant440_1103.ppt.

Chapter 6: The Opportunity

1   John D. Rockefeller as quoted in quotation examples for definition of "Would rather," copyright 2014 FineDictionary.com, http://www.finedictionary.com/Would%20rather.html.

2   Proverbs 23:7 (NASB).

Chapter 8: Action Step 4: Move the Train

1   Napoleon Bonaparte, *Napoleon in His Own Words: From the French of Jules Bertaut*, as translated by Herbert Edward Law and Charles Lincoln Rhodes (Chicago: A.C. McClurg & Co., 1916), p. 52.

Chapter 9: Action Step 5: Lay Train Tracks

1   Robert Kiyosaki, *Rich Dad's CASHFLOW Quadrant* (Plata Publishing, 2011).

2   See www.physics.stackexchange.com/questions/4831/how-long-would-a-lever-have-to-be-to-move-the-planet-earth.

Chapter 10: Right Wall, Right Ladder

1   Henry David Thoreau, *Walden; or, Life in the Woods* (Boston: Ticknor and Fields, 1854).

2   Benjamin Franklin, as quoted in "Stop Procrastinating: 5 Tips from Benjamin Franklin" by Samuel B. Bacharach, *Inc.*, last updated Jan. 31, 2013, copyright 2014 Mansueto Ventures, http://www.inc.com/samuel-bacharach/stop-procrastinating-five-tips-from-ben-franklin.html.

ACKNOWLEDGMENTS

Since 1992, I have been blessed with the most amazing wife whose love, encouragement, and patience have made my book writing possible. Laurie Woodward is without a doubt the greatest encourager and believer in my ideas, and I could not do what I do without her.

I would also like to give a special thanks to John Stahl-Wert for assisting this recovering engineer with the fictional storyline in this book. Simply stated, without his contributions, this book would not have seen the light of day.

I would also like to give a special thank you to Chris Brady for his numerous edits in taking this book from good to great. I could not ask for a better friend and business partner. In addition, Tim Marks, Claude Hamilton, Dan Hawkins, Bill Lewis, and George Guzzardo contributed through their Bradford-like leadership example. Leaders of this caliber make my role in LIFE Leadership a true labor of love.

Furthermore, the talented cast of characters at Obstaclés Press, under the leadership of Rob Hallstrand and including Norm Williams, Michelle Turner, Bill Rousseau, Deborah Brady, and many others, has made the entire publishing process stress-free.

Last but certainly not least, I would like to thank my Lord and Savior Jesus Christ for saving a ruined sinner desperately in need of His grace. Anything achieved in my life is due to His grace, love, and direction.